EQUIPPED TO PRAY

PROPHETIC INTERCESSION

Kathy Dorrell

TRILOGY CHRISTIAN PUBLISHERS

Tustin, CA

TRILOGY
A wholly owned subsidiary of TBN

Trilogy Christian Publishers
A Wholly Owned Subsidiary of Trinity Broadcasting Network
2442 Michelle Drive
Tustin, CA 92780

Equipped to Pray: Prophetic Intercession

For information, address Trilogy Christian Publishing
Rights Department, 2442 Michelle Drive, Tustin, CA 92780.

Trilogy Christian Publishing/ TBN and colophon are trademarks of Trinity Broadcasting Network.

For information about special discounts for bulk purchases, please contact Trilogy Christian Publishing.

Trilogy Disclaimer: The views and content expressed in this book are those of the author and may not necessarily reflect the views and doctrine of Trilogy Christian Publishing or the Trinity Broadcasting Network.

10 9 8 7 6 5 4 3 2 1

Library of Congress Cataloging-in-Publication Data is available.

ISBN 979-8-89333-842-3

ISBN 979-8-89333-843-0

Dedicated to my family who loves and cheers me on, to those special friends who would not let this book go unwritten, and to the Lord who is forever faithful to me.

Contents

Preface

Prayer is a simple act but one of profound mystery. Most of us start praying by just talking to God or responding to the Bible verses we read. But many believers struggle to have meaningful prayer. The kind of prayer that makes them light in their spirit and to feel strong again. I was blessed to have a mother who prayed a lot, and she modeled it for us. But I also know that God passes these gifts down to us. Nevertheless, I believe it can be modeled and taught. Prayer is one of these disciplines that we need to hear and experience. The Holy Spirit, who has been sent to teach us all things, certainly makes it easier, but if we do not know what to listen for, we can go years praying and never really encounter God. It is my hope that this book will help us connect the dots in life and make sense of how the Lord teaches us to pray and how we can partner with Him to pray according to His will.

My earliest memory of prayer is as a child sitting outside my mother's bedroom door listening to her pray. There was such a powerful presence felt even on the other side of the door. I remember hearing my mother on the phone as news of an aunt having been rushed to the hospital due to a stroke was being discussed and how I had this overwhelming pull to go pray in secret for a woman I had never met. I was only about seven years old when this happened. I remember reading my Bible and I just knew to pray the words back to God. I truly thought every believer had these experiences and that we all prayed with the same understanding. It was only when I was a young adult and going to college that I realized other believers did not pray the same way. When I was an adult, I realized that many friends had never seen prayer modeled or practiced, but rather when they asked about prayer, everyone just said, "Talk to God like you would a friend." There is some truth to this statement, but it won't necessarily produce powerful prayers when ultimately prayer is about letting God talk to you and then learning to respond back to Him. In prayer, the Holy Spirit tells us what to pray, and when we learn to pray it back to God, we find prayer to be much easier and more powerful. It is my hope to share with you some of the things I have learned about prayer from the Holy Spirit and where in Scripture these things are found. It is always a good idea to see how the Lord teaches us by His Spirit and that the Word of God explains it so well.

I want to express how prayer is part of the discipline and journey of knowing God. It is the place where we see, hear, and know that He has great plans for us and those plans are to prosper us and not to harm us. We can ask Him questions and learn how His ways are not our ways. We can see where we have been deceived and repent. We can learn the truth and find freedom. Prayer is the schoolhouse of learning about ourselves and God. Prayer is the boardroom of decision-making and the strategy room for waging war on the enemy. We can have the right answers, the right decisions, and the victories if we understand how to align with God and see His kingdom come.

This book came about from students who came asking for help in their prayer lives. As one of the pastors at Global School of Supernatural Ministry, our students hear me pray. It has been common for many of them to seek out meetings with me and desire for them to deepen their prayer lives. I began meeting with them individually but could not maintain all the individual appointments, so a prayer meeting with teaching was established as an elective. It ran for about five years before the Lord told me to stop, take all of the teaching material, and write a book. This has been a journey and one that I was not looking for, but it found me. I have been able to help students understand the ways that God speaks to them whether it is in a vision, a passing thought, or a dream. Through these years of training students to pray, I have held to a simple model and hope to explain that through this book. I believe that the Word of God and the Holy Spirit together, teach us to pray. The unity and consistency of Word and Spirit empowers us to be transformed in our prayer lives and then we can truly change the world around us. Jesus prayed often, and when He stepped out after prayer, He knew what the Father wanted Him to do. God is still faithful to lead us if we make time to listen, learn, and obey Him. May this book impact your life the way it has many of our school students. God wants us to have strong prayer lives because He knows it is the transformative lifeline for every believer.

CHAPTER ONE

Kings Dream and Prophets Pray

"And it shall come to pass afterward, that I will
pour out my spirit upon all flesh; and your sons and
your daughters shall prophesy, your old men shall
dream dreams, your young men shall see visions."
(Joel 2:28, ESV)

I grew up with a spirit-filled mom, and one of the things I will always remember about her is the way she prayed. It was full of confidence, love, and power. Every morning, and while she was doing household chores, my mother would sing, praise, and pray. Prayer was modeled; it was normal, and it was part of life. There was nothing too big or too small to pray about or to expect from God. As children, we were fascinated by her private prayer time. She would shut her bedroom door and for what seemed like forever, our mother could be heard praying. Sometimes in English and sometimes in a language we did not understand. She would seem fierce or quiet or happy or even sad sometimes, but we did not always know what she was praying about. This was fascinating. I remember listening at the door, but my heart was nervous as I wondered what was happening on the other side of that bedroom door. Prayer. My siblings and I certainly did understand one thing … God was in there with her. I recently found a poll taken by Barna, super interesting for many reasons, but the results on modeled prayer are what truly amazed me. Most Americans who are praying are doing so at home and alone. In fact 82 percent pray silently and by themselves.[1] This indicates that most of us do not see or hear prayer modeled unless we also grew up with a praying parent to model it every day, all day long.

The disciples heard Jesus pray and they asked, "Lord, teach us to pray, as John also taught his disciples"(Luke 11:1). This request is simple but the implication is they did not feel they knew how. I can only imagine the disciples sitting around while Jesus was praying and thinking to themselves about how His prayer must have seemed different than perhaps their own or others they had heard. Whatever Jesus was praying in Luke 11, we don't know, but we do know that it prompted the question: How do you pray? The disciples, like me as a kid outside my mom's door, heard something, felt something, and ultimately wondered how they could pray like Jesus prayed.

There is a story in the Old Testament that gives us our first example of prayer. It happens in Genesis 20. This story is about King Abimelech who has taken Sarah from Abraham, believing she is only his sister (she was his half-sister). It is after a troubling dream, which by the way is the first dream recorded in the Bible, Abimelech *returns* Sarah and questions Abraham as to why he misled him. The Lord tells Abimelech in verse 7 (emphasis mine), "Now then, return the man's wife, for he is a prophet, so that he will pray for you, and you shall live. But if you do not return her, know that you shall surely die, you and all who are yours."

So, what is happening here? We see how God intervenes to warn King Abimelech and to actually protect him from death. God, who created all life, would give a dream to a king so that he might live and not die. Then God, who speaks to us, positions a prophet, a spokesman, to speak life to the king and He calls it prayer.

You may wonder, like I did, *Why is this the first time we read about a dream, a prophet, and prayer?* Afterall, it is *not* the first time God has communicated with people nor is it the first time the people have talked to God. We know that from the beginning Adam and Eve and others talked with God. The story of people communicating with God is there from the garden of Eden. It is there when Noah gets directions from God ,and it is there when the Lord calls Abram to be Abraham. We read passages about talking to God and passages about "calling on His name." So, why are the words *dream*, *prophet*, and *pray* suddenly used after all the conversations in Genesis 1–19? These three words are all associated with revelatory gifts. A dream is a revelatory moment throughout the Bible and one that still happens today when God wants to talk to us about something important. A prophet is a spokesperson, which means a person who speaks on behalf of someone else. In this case, prophets spoke on behalf of God. And prayer is the life-giving words a spokesman speaks. When we pray to God, we are praying for life to overcome death or dead things in our own lives, and when we pray for others, we are also praying for life to come to them. Prayer is our ability to speak life in situations and circumstances where death would otherwise remain. It is a revelatory discipline practiced so that we use the creative and life-giving words that God, our Father, would use.

The Hebrew word used in this passage for *pray* is *palal*. It is a word used to mean mediate, intercede, judge, or intervene.[1] This gives us a better understanding of what the Lord is saying Abraham will do for Abimelech. He is explaining that because Abraham is a prophet, he can mediate, intercede, judge, or intervene for Abimelech's life. A prophet or a spokesman of God would know how God would mediate or intervene to give life to someone. This same idea for prayer is expressed in the Greek (*proseuchomai*) when used in the New Testament. It means to come face-to-face with God in order to petition (supplication), request, intervene, worship, and offer gratitude. The meaning sounds wonderfully familiar to Paul's directive to Timothy in his letters regarding prayer.

> 1 Timothy 2:1–4, *First of all, then, I urge that supplications, prayers, intercessions, and thanksgivings be made for all people, for kings and all who are in high positions, that we may lead a peaceful and quiet life, godly and dignified in every way. This is good, and it is pleasing in the sight of God our Savior, who desires all people to be saved and to come to the knowledge of the truth.*

Paul expresses this to Timothy with urgency, wanting all believers to pray life for all people, gaining peaceful lives and seeing God's will done in salvation and truth. Prayer is the practice and discipline of speaking life over our own situation, others, the cities we live in and the nations we love.

Jesus spoke of prayer as a secret place experience but one that needed to be according to the will of God. He instructed them to pray in such a way that others did not know what was being said and to not pray with many words. Most of what Jesus had to say about prayer focuses on these two important points. Our relationship with God allows us to be confident, full of faith, and few in words. The other is that prayer is a secret, private matter, between a person and God. It is not for others to be admired in their speech or knowledge. Jesus truly pointed to the relationship one has with the Father, Matthew 7:9 (NIV), "Which of you, if your son asks for bread, will give him a stone?" It is the heart of God to answer our prayers.

Relationship is the first part of understanding prayer. We need to be in a relationship with God. We need to understand our role as His people. The emphasis is that a powerful prayer comes out of this relationship and those in this holy relationship pray. We have instead minimized our prayers as a list of needs and wants rather than fulfilling the desire to see the will of God done. We don't have to use big words and make speeches, but rather speak life-giving words that allow for a fresh encounter. For so many, prayers are stale and boring instead of revelatory and conversational. Praying can become routine and lack authority. For those who've never prayed, it can seem boring and ridiculous until change is felt and noticed. If we step into a *palal* moment, we find that alignment takes place in our lives and in the lives of others.

This divine relationship provides access to an abundant life in Christ. We need to understand the relationship that we enter into for His glory and will. For example, when I was newly married, I had a revelatory experience about the power of covenant relationship. It was one of those stepping-out-in-faith moments. I had a check for cash and the bank had closed. So my husband, who is from a small town where everyone knows you, told me to take the check to the little market in the middle of town. He said the owner would cash it for me. I was quite skeptical because she didn't know me, and I didn't know her.

It was only in the trust I had in my husband that this would be acceptable that I entered the little market and asked if I could cash a check. The cashier looked at me with a big no on her face, but then I heard the owner from behind the counter say, "Is that Billy's wife?" I was stunned. There I stood, as Billy's wife, and no other name, as this business woman smiled at me. She turned to the cashier, approved the transaction, and in a moment, my check was cashed. It was not on my own reputation or relationship with her, but rather on the relationship my husband had with her. You see, Jesus is our husband, and we can cash a check because of Him. Our shared love for the same person caused a response that produced provision. It was authority and power that approved the cashing of my check. Our prayers are like that check. We come in obedience to His will, asking, and the power and authority of the Father produces the fruit of the prayer. Words that leave our mouth become the words of life or death. Proverbs 18:21, "The tongue has the power of life and death, and those who love it will eat its fruit."Are we not wise enough to give our words to Him in order to see life produced and death destroyed?

So let us look at the power, love, and authority that comes in this relationship with Christ. If our prayers reflect His heart, then we walk in the power, love, and authority He has. I was only able to cash a check in a small-town market because of an important relationship. My asking was the same as if my husband asked. The owner would give to me equally what she would have given to my husband. The Father hears us as we ask in the name of Jesus. It is as if Jesus is asking.

> "In that day you will ask nothing of me. Truly, truly, I say to you, whatever you ask of the Father in my name, he will give it to you. Until now you have asked nothing in my name. Ask, and you will receive, that your joy may be full" (John 16:23–24, ESV).

Our relationship provides a position in Christ. We are His friends, His bride, His bond servants, and His branches. All of these positions make us an equally yoked counterpart to Jesus. What He has is accessible to us as long as we stay in love, the first commandment. His authority is given to us in Christ so that we can make the decisions He would make. His love is given to us so we can love like He does, and His power is given to us to use in the manner in which He would use it.

All this reveals the kingdom of God, allowing His glory to fill the earth through His people who are in relationship with Him. Abraham had a relationship with God and the Lord called him a prophet. From this relationship, he was given authority to pray for the king; to see him live and not die. We are given a relationship, and from this place, we are called on to pray for others. If I may, we are still kings, queens, who dream and prophets, spokesmen, who pray but the New Testament gives us many new names to consider. There are few to consider as we prepare to pray with love, loyalty, commitment, and fruitfulness. It takes a revelation of who we are to enter into prayer.

The Bride Loves

What a great position to hold in Christ! We are called to be equally yoked, perfectly suited and in harmony with Jesus. This seems almost too good to be true. Honestly, if more of us understood *this* position, our prayers and actions would be quite amazing. A bride is one that is equal to the husband, suited for working alongside of and able to cooperate with Him because a bride has a shared life. This union called marriage eliminates the singular life and replaces it with shared goals and values. The bride is able to live a life equally fulfilling to the groom. We, like the check story I shared earlier, can access resources and make new relationships simply because of our one relationship with Christ. His authority and power, by grace, is given to aid us in fulfilling His will. His resources, by grace, are given to aid us in fulfilling His purposes. We are empowered by His Spirit to fulfill the plans of God. It is our role as bride that allows for us to have great faith and confidence in what He will do. This position of bride takes friendship to a deeper level and allows us to enter into His family where love is. Because of love, the common goal of disciple-making makes way for evangelism. We become the perfect partner. God, our Father, chose us to be a pure virgin for Christ. He promised us Christ as our one husband. The apostle Paul told the Corinthians that we were meant for one another.

> 2 Corinthians 11:2 (NIV), *"I am jealous for you with a godly jealousy. I promised you to one husband, to Christ, so that I might present you as a pure virgin to him."*

Our heavenly Father, who is most faithful, made covenants and promises a long time before and like Hosea to Gomer, He set His heart to bring the bride back into relationship as a faithful spouse. Like Abraham who sent a servant to find a wife for his son, the Lord found a bride for Christ. Like Adam was given Eve, the second Adam was given you and me. Though a bride walks in the authority and power for the household of Christ, it is love that ultimately gives meaning to the term "bride of Christ." Love is an essential part of living for and with God. We know that from the beginning, a chosen people would be set apart and called to love the Lord with all of their heart, soul, and strength. From Genesis to Revelation, we hear the words of patriarchs, prophets, kings, and disciples that resound with a call to love Him. Without love, there is not a chosen bride, and there are only prayers of meaningless words. Isaiah, Ezekiel, and Matthew all record the absence of love even though our mouths say all the right words (Isaiah 29:13; Ezekiel 33:31; Matthew 15:7–9).

Isaiah 29:13 (ESV):
And the Lord said:
"Because this people draw near with their mouth
and honor me with their lips,
while their hearts are far from me,
and their fear of me is a commandment taught by
men,

Ezekiel 33:31 (ESV):
And they come to you as people come, and they sit
before you as my people, and they hear what you
say but they will not do it; for with lustful talk in

their mouths they act; their heart is set on their gain.

Matthew 15:7–9 (ESV):
You hypocrites! Well did Isaiah prophesy of you, when he said:
"This people honors me with their lips,
but their heart is far from me;
in vain do they worship me,
teaching as doctrines the commandments of men."

These passages remind us that people can appear to love God, but their hearts reveal the truth. God sees the heart, and He knows the heart. It is our foolish nature to think we could deceive Him with words. Love is the basis for our relationship, and from love, we walk as a bride to the one Husband of all. The Lord was sent to bring us into unity with God. If we allow ourselves to unite with Him, loving Him with all of body, heart, soul, and strength, then we can pray, act, and represent Him well in every area of our lives. To be called His bride is a position of great honor and it comes with a responsibility to love Him first and then to love one another. When Jesus was asked which commandments were the most important, He responded.

Matthew 22:37–40 (NIV), *'Jesus replied: 'Love the Lord your God with all your heart and with all*

*your soul and with all your mind.' This is the first
and greatest commandment. And the second is like
it: 'Love your neighbor as yourself.' All the Law and
the Prophets hang on these two commandments."*

A bride who does not love, is not a bride. It is love
that brings union with God and it is love that compels
the Shulamite bride to go looking for the one she loves.
In Song of Songs 5:8 (NIV) she adjures the daughters of
Jerusalem, "I charge you—if you find my beloved, what
will you tell him? Tell him I am faint with love." We are
ultimately called into love. The prayers we pray are an
expression of the fullness of love.

Loyal Friends

Jesus said to them: "You are my friends if you do
what I command you. No longer do I call you servants,
for the servant does not know what his master is doing;
but I have called you friends, for all that I have heard
from my Father I have made known to you" (John 15:14–
15, ESV).

Apostle John gives us this amazing declaration from
Jesus about the relationship He has with those who
obey Him. Friends are the loyal ones. Friends are there
in good times and hard times. Jesus is clarifying obedience as an act where friends respond in agreement
with the one they love. He is saying that obedience is

not merely an act of doing what we are told but actually an ability to say or do what He would say or do because friends see things the same way. Obedience looks like unity whereas servants might obey but they do not necessarily agree. I find this interesting because we would say a servant is one that obeys the master or person of authority. Jesus says we are no longer servants because we no longer obey without knowing the reasons why. Friends are people who obey because they know what the Father wants. Our definition of obedience has to change. Obeying is not taking orders as we often perceive it but rather a response to a situation because the friend knows what would be the course of action. A friend knows what will bless his friend. The difference here is that the friend is involved in the reasons, plans, and purposes, whereas servants do not know what the plan is. Once Jesus arrived on the scene of eternity, we found Him sharing the fullness of God's plan with those we call disciples. Before this moment in time, God's people did not know or understand what the Father was doing. They may have obeyed at times but by and large, they were not friends. As a friend, we walk in knowing the good and perfect will of God that Romans 12:2 speaks of. It is because of all Jesus taught and the Holy Spirit who leads that we are able to do what He would do. Servants, who do not know the will of the Father, must wait for instructions. We who renew our minds, know His good and perfect will. So, we are able to make decisions and do His will as friends. Ultimately, a friend can be left to finish or build something because a friend knows what is needed. When Jesus ascended, He felt confident that with the Holy Spirit coming, His friends would know what to do and how to do it.

We need the Holy Spirit to know God, but we also need to be transformed in our minds and become His friend.

> "Do not conform to the pattern of this world, but be transformed by the renewing of your mind. Then you will be able to test and approve what God's will is—his good, pleasing and perfect will" (Romans 12:2, NIV).

Committed Bond Servant

I know I just explained that we are friends not servants, so I must explain the position of bond servant. The early church understood slavery and servants. Jesus told parables that included servants and slaves. Peter called himself servant and apostle of Christ Jesus (1 Peter 1:1), and Paul refers to bond servants, whether encouraging them to gain their freedom or not, he promotes them as equals in Christ. We can see through this a common thread—*earthly position is not the same as the position a believer has in Christ.* For many living in the

Roman Empire, this would have been challenging. The mystery of equality for all in Christ went against culture in Paul's day just as much as it does today.

> 1 Corinthians 7:21–24 (ESV), *"Were you a bondservant when called? Do not be concerned about it. (But if you can gain your freedom, avail yourself of the opportunity.) For he who was called in the Lord as a bondservant is a freedman of the Lord. Likewise he who was free when called is a bondservant of Christ. You were bought with a price; do not become bondservants of men. So, brothers, in whatever condition each was called, there let him remain with God."*

Paul explains to the early believers that a bond servant was one that now followed Christ Jesus. He was the master, and our earthly positions were irrelevant compared to the equal value of human beings. The servant was free and the free was a servant. However, he encouraged all slaves to gain natural freedom if possible. We know that he encouraged Onesimus to return to Philemon and then pleaded his case that he return "no longer as a bond servant but more than a bond servant, as a beloved brother" (Philemon 1:16, ESV). Paul recognized that it would be good for Onesimus to return and serve as a brother, not a slave. This is the concept of bond servant as defined by Paul. It is one that willingly serves his brother.

Paul is taking away the mindset that we are slaves or servants without a will. But he is rather saying that those in Christ serve Him willingly and therefore serve others. Galatians 5:13 (ESV) puts it this way, "For you were called to freedom, brothers. Only do not use your freedom as an opportunity for the flesh, but through love serve one another." It was a pleasure for Paul to call himself a servant of Christ Jesus because he realized the position was a willingness to follow Him and to see the plans of the King of kings fulfilled. All the biblical references from the disciples referring to themselves as servants of Christ is with the mindset of a willingness to follow Him. It can be likened to that of David and his mighty men. While David was in a cave and called to be king, the mighty men found him and offered their support. They were not forced or made to serve but rather recognized that David was king and the call for him to be king was worth supporting. Our prayers reflect this heart to serve willingly as we pray for our King Jesus' will to be done on earth as it is in heaven. All of us in Christ made equal and willingly giving our lives to see Him revealed in greatness and glory.

Fruitful Branches

The concept of branches brings to mind the stretching out and the sense of freedom yet still very much attached to the vine. I like the idea a lot, but then again,

I was a kid that climbed trees and sat on the branches looking out from a high place where the perspective allowed me to see the world around me very differently. Branches are the people who stay attached to the One that brings *life*. After all, it was Jesus, who said, "I am the vine; you are the branches. If you remain in me and I in you, you will bear much fruit; apart from me you can do nothing" (John 15:5). I am sure He was helping them to understand that nothing in life can last if it is not rooted in the original design of the plant. Life expectancy of any living organism is only temporary with a bit of water. Jesus would more than keep us alive temporarily; He would give us eternal life. Whereas branches can spread and grow, they only enhance and cause the vine to produce more fruit. We, like these branches, grow, spread out, and produce fruit. Our fruit only enhances and causes the whole plant, the whole vine, to prosper. Branches are an extension of who Christ is. When we grasp this understanding of our identity, we can feel freedom to grow and to create. Branches are uniquely free and yet receive nutrients and life from the source, the vine.

When I consider true friends in my life, I recall times when my best friend responded just like I would. The trust and confidence that she would take care of a matter the same way was comforting; allowing me to be at rest. It occurs to me that friendship with God might just be the place where we build trust with God. There was a time when my husband and I were away and the house we owned in our hometown suffered flooding in the basement. This was not a usual thing, so when it happened, we were not expecting that all of our stored boxes and keepsakes would be at risk. In fact, they were ruined. My best friend and her husband went to my house to check out the damage. They cleared the basement, sucked up the water, threw away what needed to go, and preserved in new plastic boxes what could be saved. All I had asked of her was to go to my house and check out the damage so I would know if I needed to come home. But instead, she took care of everything just as if it were her home. It is like this with God. Jesus went into heaven but He left us to spread the good news. When we respond as if it were our own, then we truly honor Him. In return, He can trust us and be confident that we will handle those important matters entrusted to us.

In our prayer life, this becomes important as we pray for the creative strategies, ideas, and transformation to manifest in us and the world around us. The branches become lives lived on all the cultural mountains, causing new ideas and growth. We can appear to the world as wildly unique and independent, but in reality, we are all rooted in Him. We are producing fruit and revealing His kingdom.

As we learn to pray, it takes understanding our relationship to God. If Abraham could pray a prayer of life and King Abimelech could dream dreams that warned him of danger, then most certainly with the Holy Spirit and the position we have today in Christ Jesus, we can pray powerful prayers. It takes understanding the voice of the Holy Spirit and knowing how God is talking to us. It takes finding our identity in Him and realizing we can learn His ways because the Holy Spirit came to teach us everything Jesus taught. We come into prayer with an understanding that God wants to talk to us, and He wants to help us understand His ways. When Jesus would go off alone to pray, He always came back to do the will of His Father and so can we. Jesus told us in John 5:19 that He only does what He sees the Father doing. Prayer can be the place we get to see Him and His ways. It is the place where we see that His words, in us, bring life.

CHAPTER TWO

Obedience Is Agreement

"Whatever you ask in my name, this I will do,
that the Father may be glorified in the Son."
(John 14:13, ESV)

With an intimate relationship at the center of our prayers and confidence in God to provide, protect, help, deliver, rescue, and redeem, we enter into the ultimate place in prayer and that is agreeing with Him. Again, consider your closest loving relationships and think about goals you have in common. What if you did not agree? How much of your goal would you truly achieve if you cannot agree? We must be in agreement with God in order to pray according to His will. We need to first accept that His will is truth, and we do not always know the truth.

Throughout the Bible, the phrase "according to His will" is repeated quite often. As we read the Bible, we learn that something new is revealed to us every time we read, so we keep reading. The more we study the Bible, the more we see revelatory truth and hidden mysteries. I am not sure when, but at some point, this little phrase, "according to His will," jumped off the page for me. It caused questions for me. Was I agreeing with God? Were my prayers according to His will? This all started to stir in me at a time when I was praying for my mom to heal from cancer. I was asking for healing, but she died. It was quite troubling to me to think that this would be God's will. I couldn't understand how God could let her die. I was faithful in asking, and I believed He could heal her. It was in this time of grief that I realized we start to rationalize. My belief in God's power to heal was overtaken by a belief that He must have wanted her to die. I certainly cannot say why some people recover and heal while others do not, but I can say that my mother didn't want to live anymore. She was in too much pain. God's will is to give life. Just like with Abraham, God wanted to give King Abimelech life.

We, like Abraham, are called to pray for life. But ultimately, God will decide on what is good, and if there is a loss, He will vindicate us. My loss was not meant to diminish God's will for life. This is where we get ourselves into trouble and start forming beliefs about God and His will. So I want to say first that it is best to not attribute God's will based solely on experiences but rather to form our knowledge of God from Scripture. The Word of God is truth, and the truth is that we do not always understand His will.

Our prayers and relationship with Him will lack agreement if we form ideas about God that are not true. We pray out of what we expect. If all I expect is the doctor to perform the surgery well, then all I know to pray is that surgery goes well. If I expect God to heal supernaturally, either with the involvement of doctors or no doctor at all, then I will pray for supernatural healing to come. It is in the Bible that we see Him and start to understand who He is, how He responds, and what He wants to do. Jesus models the Father, and He completely represents His heart, His will. In fact, we see even in the garden of Gethsemane that Jesus, who is praying and under a great deal of stress, says to the Father, "My Father, if it be possible, let this cup pass from me; nevertheless, not as I will, but as you will" (Matthew 26:39, ESV). He is clearly wanting to not be arrested and killed, but He is also fully aware that it is the Father's will that matters the most. He is certain the will of God is good. We, on this side of the cross, would agree. It was good that Jesus died. The Father would bring Him back to life three days later. Today, I know, my mother, though she died, is in heaven and one day, the Father will also resurrect all of those who are, as the Bible says, asleep.

All of our experiences need to be measured by truth and regardless of whether we see breakthroughs or not, we hold fast to the will of God. We pray for life; we speak the truth, and we live according to His ways. This is an agreement, a covenant relationship, a bond between friends, and true obedience to One we love.

I know there is grace as we are developing a history through relationship with the Lord. We may pray out of emotions, fears, love, and lack of understanding. I think of the disciples who in Luke 9 want to call down fire because of the Samaritans who rejected Jesus. Their personal feelings, as most Jews, towards Samaritans leaked into their perspective and created a desire to pray against them. Jesus turns to them and rebukes the idea of praying for fire to come down and consume them.

He says to James and John, *"You do not know what kind of spirit you are of. For the Son of Man did not come to destroy the lives of men, but to save them"* (Luke 9:56). I thank God for His grace that allows me time to grow and learn. My own prayer life has grown, and I have learned that the most effective prayers are those that are according to His will. It is best to not speak at all until I know how to agree with Him. Sometimes this just falls out of my mouth as I submit to His will as I know it. The Holy Spirit who helps us know how to pray will remind me of verses I have read over the years,, and He helps me stick to the truth. These verses come to my heart and mind, and I see how they apply even in today's situations. Suddenly the Bible is relevant. The Word of God is really living and sharper than a two-edged sword. I love that the Word of God is compared to a sword; one that I just need to know how to wield effectively.

Agreeing with the Word of God does require knowing the Bible and allowing God to write it on our hearts. This agreement is where the power and authority come from when we pray. The problem with many of our unanswered prayers is that we are still praying according to our own will and not His. This is the greatest challenge in our prayer lives. Who's will are we praying?

I remember in college praying for a dating relationship to work out. I was dating someone that I was more in love with than he was with me, or at least it felt that way. I wanted a commitment, and he was not ready for a committed relationship. I was praying God would work it all out because love was involved. However, I didn't understand at the time that sex, though I knew it was wrong, should not be part of this relationship. I was asking God to bless an unholy relationship. God cannot do that. He won't do that. Sometimes we pray for things that seem right—love is good, right? But unholy is unholy and God does not *will* unholy.

However, I would later repent for the unholy relationships, and I found myself praying something like this, "Lord, I am really bad at this, and I need You to choose a husband for me. I cannot be unmarried because I confess that it is true, I cannot control myself and You said it is better to get married than to fall into sin." Three months later, I began a healthy, pure relationship and each night I asked the Lord, "What am I doing?" I was so sure my past experiences would repeat and this relationship too would fail. During this time, the Lord was teaching me to repent, renew my mind, gain new experiences, and to see that He was good. I would hear the Lord say to me every time I questioned Him, "Just keep dating him." I married my husband a year later. God's will is holy. His will is truth.

We must first discover His will so that we can align and agree with Him. This is where we come back to the prophet who prayed what we looked at in Genesis 20. Prophets were spokespeople who heard God and spoke on His behalf. We need to know what God would say about a situation or a person so that we can pray like He would. It is only in trusting His leadership that we become united in one mission, one goal, one life.

Our whole lives become transformed, seeking the presence of God on earth so that the whole world experiences His love and restoration. We usher His will in with prayers of agreement. It is important that we develop the strength to pray for what is true even if we won't see it in our day. There are many seasons that our lives pass through and in each one the Lord teaches us to pray according to His will. This life of prayer becomes mysterious, and we don't fully understand how it even matters. But we do know that without prayer, nothing happens at all. It is in these moments all selfishness is diminished and we only agree with what God is doing.

Our will diminished, and His will done on earth. Every agreement is obedience to His will, allowing us to find ourselves in unity with God and with one another. If we can come to agreement, we move in the power and authority from our Father who backs up what we ask for in His name. Jesus, who embodied God in every way, prayed for us and is still interceding for us. Jesus knew the Father and He was aligned with Him, so that what He prayed for would be done on earth for us because it was the will of God. We see the fullness of intercession as Jesus intervenes on our behalf and becomes the sacrifice for all mankind. True intercession is going to the Father for the sake of others. If you have ever prayed for someone other than yourself, you have interceded.

> Romans 8:34 (NIV), *"Who then is the one who condemns? No one. Christ Jesus who died—more than that, who was raised to life—is at the right hand of God and is also interceding for us."*

Jesus, who intervened. Jesus, who is still interceding for us, demonstrated intercession. However, I want to point out that the term intercessor is not one of the roles given in the Bible, but it is an action that people, who are in close relationship to God, do. Perhaps we just needed a way to describe all those old ladies who gathered to pray for revival or that one or two that met faithfully to pray and the Spirit fell. Regardless of why we call praying people intercessors, I want to help recapture true intercession.

To intercede or make intercession comes by the Spirit to pray according to the heart of God. We have limited intercession to a list of needs and requests. Whereas it is not about our lists but rather about God's plan. True intercession is praying for God's will to be accomplished. Intercession is serving the heart of God. Lists are fine as long as they leave room for God to direct how to pray for those needs and wants. Intercession requires a person to be fully equipped to pray according to the will of God.

In the Old Testament, a long story of people called by God is modeled for us in the natural world. It is among these mighty men and women we see fathers, mothers, judges, priests, prophets, and royalty. Everyone has a role and a function to match it. It is only in the New Testament that we discover the mystery of Christ is salvation for all people. We discover that a born-again experience is available by the Spirit ,and we can actually be born again by the work of the Holy Spirit. What a wonderful realization when you've lived just long enough to know that your spirit is where life truly comes from. So how do these two testaments come together? All of these previous roles and functions suddenly become one new man. The born-again believer functions in all of these roles that were previously separated.

> "But you are a **chosen people, a royal priesthood, a holy nation, God's special possession,** that you may declare the praises of him who called you out of darkness into his wonderful light" (1 Peter 2:9, NIV, emphasis mine).

> "For you can **all prophesy** in turn so that everyone may be instructed and encouraged" (1 Corinthians 14:31, NIV, emphasis mine).

> "Do you not know that the Lord's people will judge the world? And if you are to judge the world, are you not competent to judge trivial cases? Do you not know that we will judge angels? How much more the things of this life!" (1 Corinthians 6:2–3, NIV).

As born-again believers, we become new in Christ and take on functions of a chosen people. We are royalty. We are priests. We are a prophetic people. We are able to judge and discern His ways from the ways of the world.

This means our prayers can carry different purposes and tones. We intercede from the role in which we understand the situation. A priest may come asking for mercy but a prophet comes with a declaration from the Lord. The royalty come seeking favor and provisions to fulfill the plan, and the judges cry for the Lord to move in justice, power, and love. This new position we have in Christ allows us to co-intercede with Him as well as co-labor with Him. We are a people who are now looking for all the ways to bring heaven to earth because that is what the Father wanted as prophets proclaimed that all the earth would be filled with His glory.

There is a story in the Old Testament that reveals a spiritual law, and we get a glimpse of how powerful agreement really is and how God desires unity for good and not for evil. How we agree and what we agree with matters if we want to see His kingdom come. It is the story of the Tower of Babel in Genesis 11. We need to first understand the sequence of events: the earth is destroyed by a flood because of the great evil that has spread, but God has a plan. He saves Noah and his family, who take up the first commandment known to reproduce and fill the earth. In Genesis 10 we see that this family has grown, and the Lord is sending them out across the earth to fill it. It is reminiscent of the desire of the Lord back in the garden of Eden. However, in chapter 11, we see that man does not want God's will but rather they desire to build their own kingdom, their own city.

> Now the whole earth had one language and the same words. And as people migrated from the east, they found a plain in the land of Shinar and settled there. And they said to one another, "Come, let us make bricks, and burn them thoroughly." And they had brick for stone, and bitumen for mortar. Then they said, **"Come, let us build ourselves a city and a tower with its top in the heavens, and let us make a name for ourselves, lest we be dispersed over the face of the whole earth"** (Genesis 11:1–4, ESV, emphasis mine).

It is important to understand that the earth and its inhabitants had one language and shared the "same words." This implies that they agreed with one another. They spoke the same in word and meaning. They did not want to be dispersed over the earth, but rather wanted to build their own city. They essentially wanted their way or their will to be done.

The Lord comes down to see the city they are building.

Can you imagine God coming to see the plans of mankind and taking note that the people He created are continuing to disobey rather than trusting His good plans to fill the earth with people? Why are they so adamant about staying put rather than receiving the earth as a gift from God?

> And the LORD came down to see the city and the tower, which the children of man had built. And the LORD said, "Behold, they are **one people, and they have all one language**, and this is only the beginning of what they will do. And **nothing that they propose to do will now be impossible for them**. Come, let us go down and there confuse their language, so that they may not understand one another's speech." So the LORD dispersed them from there over the face of all the earth, and they left off building the city (Genesis 11:5–8, ESV, emphasis mine).

As we read on, it becomes clear that the spiritual law of oneness is powerful. The Lord says they are "one people" and "one language," which will allow the impossible to become possible. This is an extraordinary thought to ponder. We are created to be one because there is power to do the impossible. However, God has to redirect them in order to fulfill His will in filling the earth with people. He gives them many languages and is therefore able to disperse them on the earth, accomplishing His will.

But later in the New Testament, we catch the restoration of God's heart for unity. Jesus cries out for oneness in the garden of Gethsemane and asks the Father to make us one.

> "I do not ask for these only, but also for those who will believe in me through their word, that **they may all be one**, just as you, Father, are in me, and I in you, that they also may be in us, so that the world may believe that you have sent me." (John 17:20–21, ESV)

The coming of the Holy Spirit at Pentecost causes the disciples to speak in many languages allowing the city to receive the gospel in their own language!

> "And at this sound the multitude came together, and they were bewildered, because each one was hearing them speak in his own language" (Acts 2:6, ESV).

By giving us His Holy Spirit, He creates unity again, but this time it allows the disciples to preach to everyone from all over the known world in the language they understand. Immediately the gospel goes forth. What had been an impossible commission became totally possible through one language that others could understand.

The takeaway in these parallel stories is the unity and common language of God. We were meant to agree with Him, His plans, His ways, and His people. It is disobedience that brings disunity. By the Holy Spirit, we learn His heart, His thoughts, His ways and are transformed into people who are able to obey and follow Christ.

Agreement with God is where powerful prayer lives erupt and breakthroughs happen like a glimmer of light in a dark room. It is the place where trouble is resolved, and problems bow to Jesus. Truth is every word that God speaks, and when we learn to pray the truth, we find heaven and earth collide.

CHAPTER THREE

Mindsets of Prayer

*"For my thoughts are not your thoughts, neither
are your ways my ways, declares the LORD."*
(Isaiah 55:8, ESV)

A mindset is the established attitudes or thought
processes we have because of previous experiences and
lessons taught to us. Depending on our mindset, we
could be praying in agreement with God, or we might
be striving in prayer for our own way. Not only does
Isaiah declare the conflict between our thoughts and
the thoughts of the Lord, but so do the Psalmist, apostle Paul, and other prophets. It seems to be a constant
theme and plea of the Lord that we would understand
His ways. Afterall, it does make it easier to work in
unity when we see things the same way. A mindset will
determine our confidence and willingness, all of which
affects how we come to God. If I am not sure that it is
His will, how could I ask with confidence?

Jesus gave His first sermon on a mountain. Matthew chapter 5 calls it just that, Sermon on the Mount. It is here that Jesus begins to address the established attitudes, and we call them the Beatitudes today. He redefines who the kingdom is for by listing off the perspectives of the everyday person. My point is that our attitudes and mindsets determine how we see the kingdom, the world, and therefore affect how we pray.

I am a mother of four great children. However, raising them, like most families, has not always been the easiest. I remember trying to put shoes on them, urging them to put shoes on in a timely manner so we could get out the door. The moments when they cooperated certainly went faster than wrestling with them. Isn't it always like this? When we are working for the same goal, we get more accomplished. It is like this with the Father. When we can see or understand His ways, we are more likely to unify and cooperate with Him. It is in our own way of thinking that we hold up His plans and try doing things our own way.

Nevertheless, our faithful Father and redeeming Savior always redirects and helps us to eventually get to the place we are supposed to be.

The apostle Paul writes to the Romans, Ephesians, and Philippians to "renew your minds." He is constantly reminding them that their thoughts need to be renewed so that they can follow God's ways and heart.

He wants His spiritual children to obey the Lord. It will make impossible become possible as well as transforming the world they live in. A few of the benefits of God's will are revealed in the passages Paul writes to these new believers:

> Romans 12:2 (NIV), *"Do not conform to the pattern of this world, but be transformed by the renewing of your mind. Then **you will be able to test and approve what God's will is**—his good, pleasing and perfect will."* (emphasis mine)

> 2 Corinthians 10:5 (NIV), *"We demolish arguments and every pretension that sets itself up against the knowledge of God, and we take captive every thought to make it **obedient** to Christ.*

Obedience comes easier when we think like He thinks. His will is defined as good, pleasing, and perfect. So, how does this affect how we pray? Polling and statistics show that most Americans pray but when and why is where it gets really interesting. Most pray solo and silently (82 percent).[2] The polls, however, show that prayer is mostly thanksgiving or need based with an almost equal percentage either way (62 percent thanksgiving and 61 percent needs).[3] What is equally important to note is that prayer for the world or nations' concerns are only about 20 percent of why we pray.[4] My point is this: our mindset of prayer is currently what benefits us or is personal to us rather than what is beyond us and for all the people of God. We fall short on praying for the world that He "so loved." But the Lord of our journey is so very patient, and He works to get us to a place of learning His ways. Whether it is need-based prayer, crisis moments, or worship times, the Holy Spirit is teaching us to pray!

Need-Based Mindset

It all begins by calling on the name of the Lord. This concept precedes the first use of the word *pray* mentioned early. It is one of the first concepts of prayer, but it is a secret and adoring way to relate to God. Jesus offers this also as a way to pray when He says, "Our Father, who is in heaven, hallowed be Your name" (Matthew 6:9, NASB). Calling on the name of the Lord is a recognition of who He is and how you and I humbly seek Him.

It is the understanding that He is revered, honored, above all, and we are aligning ourselves with His power and person. In fact, this phrase is used on every occasion where an altar is built, an offering is given, worship is offered, and people are grouped by His name. It is by calling on His name, we begin to seek God. This is the turning point and testimony of a person or people group who now seek Him when they previously did not, or it is in a moment when the person or group realizes a greater understanding of God that causes them to align themselves with Him in a deeper way. In fact, the New Testament Greek word for "call on" is *epikaleo* and one of the meanings of this is to take on the surname of the one you are aligning with. This is significant because most of us remember when our lives turned to God or repenting brought us closer. It is in those moments that we are actually calling on the name of the Lord. The first time we read this phrase "calling on the name of the Lord" is in Genesis 4:26 when Seth's son Enosh is born. Seth, of course, is the son who follows after Abel's death and is the son whose family line would eventually lead to the Messiah. Cain's family line, though some may have turned to the Lord, were by all accounts turning away from God. This calling on His name is the foundation of repentance and following the Lord as His people, carrying His name. This repentance is the greatest need of all people. Carrying His name is our greatest honor. The apostle Paul put it this way in Romans 10:13 (ESV): "Everyone who calls on the name of the Lord will be saved." This is for all nations and all people. Paul is, in the context of this verse, clarifying that there is no longer Jew or Gentile, and the Lord is the Lord of all. When we call on His name, we are in return called by His name.

2 Chronicles 7:14 (NKJV), *"If My people who are called by My name will humble themselves, and pray and seek My face, and turn from their wicked ways, then I will hear from heaven, and will forgive their sin and heal their land."*

Most of our stories with God begin with a prayer of repentance, getting right with Him. We come to the Lord seeking this universal need. Then we come with all our needs recognizing that He is able to help us. From this position of humble need, we begin to trust and develop faith that God will indeed do what we acknowledge He is able to do. For some this may be a little or a lot of faith. Our relationship is need based. It is truly not unlike a newborn needing a parent.

This doesn't mean we are absent of love for Him or blind to the love He has for us, but our newfound understanding of how much we need Him leads us to pray. In fact, this is why so many believers pray when going through difficult times whereas prayer takes a back seat when life is going well. When we believe that we can handle life or that everything is good, it becomes less likely we feel that we need God. It is the reason Jesus said the rich would find it difficult to enter the kingdom of God. Our prayers and communication with God have to come from a place of first understanding that we need Him. He is indeed life and apart from Him, there is no life. Ecclesiastes is very clear that everything is meaningless without God as it will all come to nothing. Our first prayer is that of calling on His name, humbly recognizing our needs.

> John 14:6, *"Jesus said to him, 'I am the way, the truth, and the life. No one comes to the Father except through me.'"*

I am convinced that our foundation of prayer really begins here in this place of knowing that we are not fully able to live abundant lives apart from Him. We start to see that only Jesus can bring truth and life back to us. I was and am still a person who wants to understand others. I have always been intrigued with how people treat one another and why they make the decisions they do.

Growing up, my mother loved the Lord, but my father did not. In fact, he admittedly told us on more than one occasion. I saw the neediness in our family, and I learned from my mom that we needed God to help us, protect us, and to provide for us. God became known to me as a helper, protector, and provider. This is important because we will always pray to Him based on how we know Him. She was great at pointing to Him for everything. We fully understood that our mom was in the same battles we were, and the only way out was God. And I am pleased to say that our victories and survival was due Him. We were all in the same oppressive situation, and my mother was leading the charge in prayer to the only One who could help. She needed to stay alive, literally, and was willing to stand in the gap for all of her children. Telling her whole story might be for another book and another day, but in this instance, I simply want to show that out of our needs, we can develop powerful prayer lives.

My mother prayed for our safety. Some of my earliest memories are ones that we can all relate to as it is quite common for children to wake up at night scared of the dark. The house we lived in was scary and it was full of darkness.

This darkness wasn't simply the absence of sunlight or a light in a room; it was obvious that our house had some dark influences. I shared a room with two of my sisters. We all slept in a queen-size bed together. In the winter, when it was cold, this was a blessing. I mention this because when a child wakes in the night, scared, it doesn't matter how many sisters are sleeping right next to you. My mom would say, "When you're scared, pray; Jesus will come and whatever is scaring you will go away." She knew our protection was in Jesus. She couldn't completely protect us from darkness, but Jesus could. She taught us this. I knew that whatever was lurking, seen or unseen, Jesus was the one to protect us.

I still pray this way every time I wake up at night. I have taught my children the same lesson. It doesn't mean that I don't allow them to come running to my room if they need me, but I know that if each one learns to go to the Lord, they will always know where their true protection comes from. This will outlast me.

My natural father was extremely abusive and sometimes my mother took the brunt of it. This happened sometimes during the day, but I recall many nights waking up to her crying while violence raged downstairs. I lay in bed listening and praying that the Lord would keep her alive. Sometimes, we prayed from our bedrooms; other times we sat in the woods behind our house and prayed together for her. I even hid in a closet one time and prayed that she would be safe. All of these prayers of protection were in the secret place. No one would have known; no corporate meeting was called to order and no talk about it afterwards followed. It was faith planted in small children that led us to pray when we were scared. My mother endured the abuse, but she lived. In time, the Lord who is patient even with abusive husbands, eventually stopped all of the abuse. We were happy that she had survived and so had we!

With the reality of nine children, my mother had to be a great cook. This was true of her and a blessing to all of us. She went weekly to the grocery store and somehow always bought enough food to feed us. As an adult now, I realize she must have had some supernatural help in this area for sure. She could cook and leftovers seemed to multiply. We never lacked food or snacks or desserts. We never lacked clothes, games, or anything we needed. I don't recall doing without, and yet I was completely aware that we were poor. I know now that she prayed daily for all of these things and her ability to wait on the Lord to provide was amazing. My mother made it part of her life to never take glory away from God.

For every meal and every item, we were made aware that the Lord provided. She would sometimes stop us while we were playing, gather us all together, and tell us how the Lord provided something. I remember once, with great excitement, she announced how the Lord brought us potatoes. Our neighbors owned a potato farm and one day, while my mother was about to make dinner, our neighbor arrived with several baskets of potatoes. She was so thrilled to see those potatoes because she had just told the Lord that morning how she had used the last of her potatoes the day before. We grew up with an understanding that our food, clothes, needs, and wants came from God.

> Matthew 6:31 (NIV), "So do not worry, saying, 'What shall we eat?' or 'What shall we drink?' or 'What shall we wear?'"

The relationship my mother had with the Lord was one of need. She needed Him to help her in life situations that she didn't have much say in. She needed Him to help her with all of her children, and in turn, she taught us all about the Lord.

I learned to pray when I was scared. I learned to pray when I needed food, clothes, or anything whether it was necessity or want. I learned that Jesus was my help in times of need, and He would take care of me. These little life lessons and the constant gratitude Mom expressed for the Lord's help overflowed in my own life. I knew that people needed God.

When children learn these basics early, it doesn't take much to see them step out on their own and we did. I remember stepping out in faith over kittens. I loved kittens when I was a child, probably because the barn cats were always pregnant and finding a kitten was as easy as finding air to breathe. I named them all and spent a lot of time taming them. All of which was not as highly valued by my parents. But I do remember having a kitten once that developed a growth of some sort on its neck. This growth was quite infected and looked rather ominous. The cat had started to look scraggly and sick, and my mother insisted I not touch it. I, on the other hand, couldn't let it die. I took oven mitts and would hold it, pet it, and pray that God would heal it. My mom would look frightful when I did this. But it didn't take much faith because she had already taught me my need for Jesus; that He provided, protected, and helped us.

Soon this cat healed, recovered, and became one of the biggest, healthiest cats we ever owned.

My mother was amazed. She told me my faith and love for the cat was the reason the Lord answered my prayers. She did not have enough faith for a cat!

This is the beginning of knowing God for most people. Our lives are in need, and we reach out to see His goodness, only to find that He is there to provide for us, to protect us, and to help us.

As I grew up, this foundational belief manifested in my life with God's help in college, relationships, jobs, and all sorts of provision. Knowing that we need Him in all areas of life grows and becomes stronger as we see the Lord break in and provide, protect, and help with all our needs. He is able to do more than we realize. May we never get to a place where we stop asking for what we need. When our needs are met, all glory goes to Him; otherwise we are in danger of letting the lack of gratitude sneak in and steal the glory for ourselves. It is important for us to understand though God provides external needs, He is also able to provide internally. He gives us new thoughts, new strategies, new plans, and new ways. All of which can drastically set us on new paths. Though this is the kind of prayer life we all start with, it is not all that prayer is meant to be. It is part of our relationship with God. Calling on Him is adoring Him, worshiping Him, and ultimately recognizing our need for Him. This is faith building, trust growing, hope filling, and love developing in our lives. It is meant to lead us to a deeper understanding and intimacy with God that truly becomes co-laboring in the Spirit. We eventually journey into praying for more than our needs. I do not believe that God causes poverty or problems to teach us that we need Him, but I can say that if more of us understood blessings, we would pray with a balanced focus on needs and gratitude. God blesses all people with everything they need. He made a whole planet that provides for us. The lack does not come from Him but rather our own inability to take care of one another. If we only pray because we lack, then God has become no more than an ATM. Though this is a beginning for many people, we cannot let our prayer lives stay in this basic foundation, reducing God to the place of when I need Him. Our prayer lives will never deepen, and we will never really have a strong relationship with God. Meeting our needs is just the beginning. It is often how the Lord reveals Himself, but need-based prayer lives are not the goal. The goal is to see who He is and to know Him to be true in the way He has been revealed to you. The goal is to cause us to become like-minded.

Crisis Mindset

Crisis is unavoidable. We live in a world full of pain and suffering; even when we try to avoid it, grief, loss, and tragedy sneak in. It is in these sudden waves of disappointment and pain that worry and fear could become rooted. But God, who is faithful, prompts us to pray.

I remember getting a phone call one evening in the early fall from a fellow teacher. She called to say that one of our peer teachers had been rushed to the hospital with an aneurysm and that we were starting a prayer chain for her. It was in this moment of crisis that a public school would start calling all the teachers and ask them to pray. I took the call, hung up the phone, and went to my bedroom. As I knelt beside the bed, and tears began to form in my eyes, I prayed one of the most simple prayers ever. "Lord, save her. Come with healing and protect her." As my heart and mind processed the impossible reality of her situation, my inner self could feel the prompting of the Holy Spirit and suddenly my tears stopped, and this inner knowing took over ... she was going to be okay. Nothing in the natural world supported the fact, but everything inside me knew she would recover. And she did!

It wasn't long prayers or perseverance for weeks on end but rather one simple moment where more than one agreed with God that she would live and not die. This was powerful and this produced a miracle in her life. Not only did she live, but she recovered mobility, speech, and life. She went through all the stages of recovery and therapy, and she returned to work and continued to teach. Within two years, this crisis was as if it had never happened.

Moments of crisis take agreement with God's heart to produce life and other believers to believe. I understand that we don't always experience miracles like this one, but nevertheless, I learned that one prayer of simple faith that partners with others as much as aligning with God's heart, produced a miracle.

I think our challenge with a crisis is the intense humanness to fight, flight, and freeze. The Barna poll mentioned earlier found that 49 percent of Americans pray because of a crisis.[5] When we are unsure of who God is and not seeing His "good, pleasing and perfect will," we can step into fear and worry. Then our prayers are not coming from agreement with God; they border on lack of faith and trust, making us doubt His will. I remember my sister who called me upset, and rightly so, to let me know that the doctors found cancer on her liver.

By the grace of God and the help of the Holy Spirit, I didn't give into that fear but rather I looked at it and responded with "Don't be afraid. We will pray every day until you go back to the doctor." For three days we prayed once a day and allowed faith and confidence in God's will to be made manifest in her body. When she went back to the doctor, they ran tests and then ran more tests. The doctor finally responded with, "I know what I saw, but it isn't there anymore." Praise God, what had been in previous tests could no longer be found. The doctor didn't know how to explain it, but he kept running tests, thinking something was wrong. She went home cancer free and has stayed cancer free.

I am not saying that every crisis goes this way, but I am saying that the way we respond and our heart alignment with who God is has power. This power can change lives if only we would use our prayers to speak truth and not give in to the fears and the limited understanding of the world. We have the opportunity in a crisis to invite God to move in power and to see Him produce miracles, making impossible fully possible.

Worship Mindset

With those statistics still in the back of our minds, I want to mention that the Barna poll of 2017 let us know that only 8 percent of Americans who pray do so because they are worshiping who God is. This is evidence that we are people who have only learned to pray when it is about us. Whereas worship is about who God is and what He wants to do. Most Christians do not learn to pray on the offensive, but rather they respond when needs or crises arise. They get defensive. Prayer is more than this. Prayer is an intentional act to partner with God for what He is doing on the earth. One of my favorite definitions of prayer comes from a sociologist, Linda Woodhead, who wrote *The Sociology of Prayer*. In it she offers this amazing definition: *"An intentional interaction ... which connects the individual or group to the supernatural, can be elicited through the process of prayer and demonstrates how believers can enter into a different reality at will."*[5] As she studied the reasons for prayer and how people use prayer, she discovered that they could be intentional and could connect to a different reality by will. This is the heart of prayer. What she may or may not realize is that this alternate reality is greater than the "temporary" world we live in. It is the eternal reality of God.

We can intentionally interact with God in the supernatural and come out of prayer with a strategy or plan that we could not have perceived within our own context. He alone has ways that are more profound. It is coming into prayer with a heart ready to acknowledge God as the authority and divine orchestrator of a good, pleasing, and perfect will.

Worship allows us to pray in thanksgiving, love, and recognition of God, of Christ, of the Holy Spirit. We worship because of who He is, and this opens us up to a reality that is far greater than what our limited experience calls logic.

A worship mindset is set on things above. It requires a new perspective.

Colossians 3:2 (ESV), *"Set your minds on things that are above, not on things that are on earth."*

When I first grasped this, I was trying to understand how God saw my life and how He felt about what I was doing in my family and my job. I was longing to understand if God cared about my job, because at the time I was struggling to see how working every day had significance. I was experiencing fatigue and tiredness trying to raise four children and keep up with a full-time job. Have you ever struggled with going to work and wondering if it was truly important? It was in this season of my life that the Lord spoke to me about perspective. It was that plane ride where I was looking out the window only to have one of those sudden moments where the Holy Spirit illuminates within us and revelation comes. I understood that everything seemed smaller when you get a perspective from above. I began asking the Lord to help me see my life from above. I wanted my mind to be set on things above. If I could see it from His perspective, then I could ask Him for it. I could see that things were much easier to understand if I knew what God was doing in my life.

Allowing ourselves to enter prayer from a place of worship helps us to partner with the Lord as the ultimate leader. Trust and faith grow in this kind of heart posture. We start to trust His ways and believe in the things we know are above.

Rather than allowing worship to simply be a forty-five-minute Sunday morning, we can intentionally worship who God is by declaring His worthiness in the secret place where no music is invading, and a holy heart speaks to the Holy God. A worship mindset causes prayer to rise above our circumstances and declare that God is able to do more than we can imagine.

CHAPTER FOUR

Body Language, Seated in Heavenly Places

*"Oh come, let us worship and bow down; let us
kneel before the LORD, our Maker."*
Psalm 95:6 (ESV)

We have talked about mindsets when it comes to how we see prayer, but there is one mindset that pertains to no words. It is the mindset of body language. We have all been in situations at work, with family, or an event somewhere and noticed others' faces, the way they sit, the way they stand, the way they pace around a room. Our body language says a lot about what we're thinking, what we're feeling, and a whole lot about the attitude we have.

Even in the Bible, we see different forms of body language. Sometimes someone may fall on their face, bow before, lay prostrate, stand and shout, maybe even rip their clothes and rub ashes on himself. Body language communicates how we feel, how we think, the way we see ourselves, and the way we see others. Think about when you meet someone really important; your body language approaches them often with honor and respect. Think about a time in your life when you didn't have a whole lot of honor or respect for someone. What was your body language then?

There are certain body language gestures that we can observe in Scripture that tell us a little bit about how the person is feeling in the presence of God. These gestures are not uncommon today; we still use them in worship, culture, and interactions with one another and most of all, we use them when we feel God near us or far away.

Hands and feet are especially mentioned throughout the Bible. These nonverbal forms of expression are used to demonstrate someone's motive or, in other words, what their heart might really be feeling. There are some examples we can look at to get an idea of these nonverbal expressions. In Ezekiel 6:11 we see God commanding the prophet Ezekiel to clap his hands and stomp his feet while he's regarding sinful Israel.

These nonverbal expressions emphasize that God, through Ezekiel, is not happy with sinful Israel and is rather angry. In the Old and New Testament, we see people giving a blessing by lifting their hands toward the group as the blessing is being spoken.

One very important thing to remember is that sometimes those hands and feet that were meant for blessing could at another time mean something else. My point in mentioning the use of gestures in various ways is because it's relative to a person or even to a culture. The culture of heaven is strange to us until the Holy Spirit leads us to understand and then we find ourselves raising a hand, bowing, or laying down as we pray.

In ancient times, we see Abraham's servant promise to find a wife for Isaac by putting his hand under the thigh of Abraham. However, later in the book of Daniel 12:7, we see raising your hand as a way of keeping a promise. In fact, Ezekiel 20:5 says that God Himself raised His hand when He made an oath, a promise. In Exodus 3:5 we see that Moses removed his shoes because the ground was holy at the burning bush. Later in Joshua 5:15 we see that Joshua also removes his shoes as a way of recognizing a holy moment. But in 2 Samuel 15:30 we see grief in removing the shoes or Deuteronomy 25 shows us that removing the shoes was a sign of disrespect, and in Ruth it's pretty clear that it is sealing an agreement. Again all of these expressions are nonverbal and they have specific meaning but the meaning is only relevant in the context of each situation.

When we are praying or worshiping, our nonverbal expressions are important. They say what words are

not saying. I discovered a long time ago that in different situations I sometimes could not feel the Lord near,
but when I seemed to be at the end of myself and allowed my body to be truthful, it was in those moments
I felt the Lord come close. This sent me on a journey
in my own prayer life to allow myself to be honest and
vulnerable before the Lord. If King David could lead a
procession naked and dancing, then there is something
definitely beautiful in the way we come before the Lord
in honesty, in reverence, in awe. Our body language is
one way to pray, to worship, to prepare ourselves to enter into holy moments with the Lord.

I remember a time when my husband and I were
part of a team church plant and in that planting, we
were also starting a Saturday night community prayer
house. It was in this prayer house one evening when I
heard the Lord prompt me, "Take off your shoes. This is
holy ground." I looked around and decided I didn't have
the courage to do that.

Every little fear of people that might look at me or
I might seem weird started to fill my thoughts. I just
couldn't bring myself to take off my shoes in church.

Then it happened! A lady in the back row walked to
the front, took the microphone and announced in the
most un-weird way, "The Lord says to take off your
shoes ... this is holy ground." I was stunned. It was like
something out of the Bible, and I was quickly led into a
search regarding the importance of our body language.

I felt confirmed and good, but I also felt bad and sad that I didn't have the courage she had, and I could have obeyed Him the first time. Now, I know that God gives us the opportunity to obey over and over so I was thankful for a second chance. I learned at this moment that I had heard the Lord correctly, and for some reason, taking my shoes off was a wordless expression I had been invited into. Body language that says He is holy. Does that mean I take off my shoes every time I worship and pray? Of course not! It is our ability to discern the appropriate body language just like we would use the appropriate words.

Within our culture and especially within our churches, most believers are not given the freedom to move around freely or to physically come before the Lord other than sit and stand. I completely understand the need for order and our responsibility to keep chaos at bay, but the pendulum that swings to no movement can actually hinder our full expression before the Lord. Keeping in mind Romans 12, which says our bodies are a living sacrifice, holy and acceptable, which is spiritual worship. Our bodies not only need to be healthy in terms of the food we eat, exercise we give them, and necessary sleep, but they are meant for worship. Sometimes our bodies need to find the position that most allows us to come to the Lord with a true and genuine heart. Consider this verse and let me challenge you in your thinking on this matter:

Ephesians 2:6 (ESV), *"And raised us up with him
and seated us with him in the heavenly places in
Christ Jesus."*

When I consider what it means to be seated in heavenly places with Christ, I understand this is symbolic of
our spiritual connection and that we are indeed with
Him as He is with us. But as I have prayed through
many seasons of joy, grief, sadness, and all the other
emotional circumstances, I understand that my body is
part of this mysterious life in Christ.

I am not physically with Christ in heaven but I can
express my seasons of life through actions and gestures
as well as words. With that said, I think it is far better to
let your body "get seated" with Christ. In other words,
it is important to remind myself and to express to the
Lord that I am aware of His position, and I desire to
align myself with Him.

When I sit with students who want to deepen their
prayer lives, I always ask them to change their physical
positions. Sometimes we sit on the floor; sometimes we
pace around the room, or we lay face down. The point
of this exercise is to find a position where you become
most honest with Christ. Aware of His nearness and
aware that you are in a position close to Him. This is
finding a place that allows us to express ourselves with
genuine feelings and this proximity helps us speak

freely and with truth. It eliminates all false ideas that we put on and pretend to have it all together.

If I were in heaven, physically, sitting next to Christ Jesus, we would talk. We would talk about life, people, the world, and I am sure He would share the plans that are being unveiled throughout time and history. Prayer is a place where we can sit with Christ and step into the kind of conversations friends might have. Friends that are sitting side by side, just talking. Perhaps dreaming of a world to come or sharing news that a friend might need to know. Learning to sit with the Lord is to lean in and listen to what He is saying about all the situations. We begin to understand His ways.

> Amos 3:7 (ESV), *"For the Lord GOD does nothing without revealing his secret to his servants the prophets."*

In this seated place with Him, the Lord reveals His secrets to His servants the prophets. Now I know that is an Old Testament verse, but even in the New Testament, we learn from the apostle Paul that "we know in part and we prophesy in part" (1 Corinthians 13:9, ESV), meaning we prophesy the things He reveals to us. This is not simply the job of a few great Old Testament prophets but rather a people filled with the Holy Spirit who can hear the Lord and repeat what He says. Prophecy does not always mean the future, but it does mean we are able to speak wisdom, clarity, and truth about God, people, and ourselves. It is gaining true understanding so that we see things from His perspective.

My point is that a follower of Christ must be close in relationship to hear the secrets the Lord wants to tell. We may only learn His ways a little at a time, but that is why we spend more time, every day, listening to the Holy Spirit as we find honest ways to get before the Lord. Our ability to enter into His presence can begin with body language, allowing ourselves to find a place where we can be vulnerable and honest with God. Then our prayers become full of His presence, and we feel confident to ask Him for anything.

When we bow, or get low, before the Lord, there is no room for pride or a false sense of strength. We acknowledge that He is worthy to bow before. We let our posture tell Him that He is worthy to fall on our face for. Fear of man or what people may think about us must disappear so that all glory goes to the Lord. Humility covers us and 2 Chronicles 7:14 becomes reality, *"If my people who are called by my name humble themselves, and pray and seek my face and turn from their wicked ways, then I will hear from heaven and will forgive their sin and heal their land."*

Learning to humble ourselves is more than words. It is first seen in the body language we use as we come before Him. Before you start praying, let yourself try out different positions and find a spot where you feel most honest, but comfortable, and it is there you have found your seat beside the Lord of Lords, who is seated in heaven.

One of the best testimonies I have heard about this was from one of my co-workers who heard me teaching on prayer. She told me the next day that during the night she woke up and knew the Lord wanted her to pray. So she thought she would try out this body language thing I had talked about in class. She told me that as soon as she lay down flat on the floor and began to pray, it was like *whoosh!* The presence of the Lord was there. It made praying so easy and simple, especially in the middle of the night.

Body language is meant to communicate our heart towards Him, not to become showy. It is not an attempt to perform for others and we cannot think that just because we express ourselves in physical ways it means we are sitting with the Lord in agreement. Jesus called the Pharisees out on performing or trying to look holy by doing things in expressive ways. We, too, need to be seeking honesty with the Lord as it would be ridiculous to think we could deceive God by simply lying face down or standing with our arms stretched out. It is our ability to know Him and to come before the Lord in a way that we fully love Him with our whole heart, mind, body, and strength.

Our ability to find our seat with the Lord is to be humble and to prepare ourselves to listen for Him. We wait on the Lord and in the waiting, we find ourselves paying attention to every sense and feeling of His presence, to passing thoughts or impressions that come to our mind and heart spontaneously. We begin to experience sudden understanding and clarity in situations that we would otherwise struggle with as talking too much only increases worry and anxiety. Then in the quiet seat before Him, we find the exact words to speak, and so prayer begins.

CHAPTER FIVE

Listening (Build a Fire, Enter the Courts)

"Call to me and I will answer you, and will tell you
great and hidden things that you have not known."
Jeremiah 33:3 (ESV)

"Call to me" is a wonderful command from the Lord. It makes me think of the sound of a loved one's voice calling my name; it immediately stops us and causes a response. It is the heart behind prayer. We are calling to Him and in return, He answers. Our God is not as silent as many might think but rather He is indeed inclined to listen and respond to us with great and unsearchable things; things we do not know. In this chapter, I will explain how to call on Him; how to listen and know that He is listening too.

I do not actually know the first time I heard the Lord or at least the first time I realized God was saying some-

EQUIPPED TO PRAY

thing to me. I was probably too young to understand and young enough to simply believe. In this world, the only kind of listening we learn is auditory, but in the Spirit, listening is not necessarily an auditory voice outside of us. It is most likely an inner small voice that may sound just like you. In other words, the Lord often speaks through our own inner voice. The difference is there is no premeditated thought but rather a spontaneous or sudden voice. It can seem almost alarming as it strikes a response from us.

I think of how the voice of God is taught to us in the Bible. First Kings 19:12 (NKJV) describes it as "a small still voice," and Samuel in chapter 3, of the first book, thinks the voice sounds like Eli. It takes Samuel four times before he realizes it is God speaking to him. It is amazing that most of the Bible describes God's voice as quite ordinary and gentle, even when Hollywood would want to overdramatize it as booming and scary.

When we are listening to God, we are measuring the calm voice, the holy voice, the wise voice, the voice of authority, and the voice of power. We hear Him just as He is in Scripture. Listening is the most useful relational tool we have when it comes to understanding people. It is also true in order to understand the ways of God.

Because our lives are full of learning and in it, we experience God more and more. It is over time that we begin to understand His voice in our lives. Whether we

65

learned to pray for forgiveness, direction, understanding, or the usual blessing, we develop ears that hear Him. But when life comes like a storm, it can get harder to hear the still small voice in all the loud chaos of life. There have been a few seasons in my life when trauma and consistent challenges were vying for my attention, so trying to block out all the noise of the day, the worries of tomorrow, and some of the haunting past mistakes seemed difficult to do. But it was in those seasons that I learned to listen the most. Hearing God in easy times is easy. Hearing God in the hard times can get confusing and difficult. Listening is essential to partnering with Him so that you can pray.

Difficulties in life can make listening seem like God isn't answering. It can be frustrating and cause us to feel like He is far away and then we do not know what or how to pray. Listening is required and babbling in uncertainty must cease. I think of it like being in a very loud emergency situation where it is difficult to take everything in and to hear the sound of the help and rescue. Instead, we become overwhelmed and we start complaining or babbling to God. We panic and worry that more tragedy is coming. Our prayers start sounding like fear and then our whole mind, body, and spirit erupt with fight, flight, and freeze. This response can hinder listening and obeying. It can cause us to partner with worry and fear. His voice is calm. Our God stays calm and calm needs to be our response so we can hear Him.

Listening is the weapon of peace, and it allows us to confidently lean on the Lord for strategy and direction as well as for comfort. Learning in the hard seasons looks like focusing my attention on Him, and it is there we find strength. Building a fire is a phrase meant only to describe focusing on the Lord. It is one way to practice getting to know God and to humbly rely on Him.

Building a Fire

God made His presence known to Israel as He led them out of slavery. He was a cloud by day and fire by night. "Building a fire" is how I start to listen for God and recognize He is near.

Let us think about building a fire in the natural world. We add one piece of wood at a time and then each breath or puff of air fans the flame. Listening looks like this. I meditate on who God is. I speak it out loud or internally, slowly. Each declaration is like throwing a stick on the fire, and in between declarations, I listen. Hearing Him begins more like a feeling of confidence that grows or courage that rises. These emotions within me reflect the character of God. For some, there may be other strong emotions that fill within but they all reflect the attributes of the fruit of the Spirit.

It is by practicing the presence of God, declaring who He is, that we learn to hear Him in the garden of our hearts. As we exalt Him, our heart, soul, and mind begin to focus on Him so much so that our whole being becomes aware of God. For me personally, I felt His presence displayed by the fruit of His Spirit. I became more aware of those attributes as if they were heightened or more prominent. But over the years, I have also felt the nearness of God when there were manifestations such as heat on my hands, legs that began to shake, or even tears that started to fall. We enter into His presence, and His presence overwhelms us. It is in these moments that we become aware of our heavenly seat as much as we are aware that the Holy Spirit lives in us. It is in recognizing who God is that we begin to reflect His image and see ourselves rightly. This, I believe, is where strength resides and confidence to ask or proclaim happens.

Instead of praying out of all the worries and fears we are experiencing, we can choose to start praising Him for who He is, and suddenly our strength and faith begin to grow. We are, in these moments, allowing ourselves to reflect the image of God. We see Him and we see ourselves. When the disciples asked Jesus to teach them to pray, He started with the phrase, "Our Father in heaven, hallowed be your name" (Matthew 6:9, ESV). In this one phrase, we see three true statements about

God. He is our father; He is in heaven, and His name is hallowed (awe).

If I were to "build a fire" based on these three truths, I would close my eyes, but only so I can focus and not because something supernatural is going on. I would find a quiet place so that again I would be able to focus on God. Then I would pray each truth slowly with pauses between each one. During the pause, I would be listening for Him. When His attributes rise up around or within, you know that He is there. It is time to listen. Listening looks like feeling His presence which is best described as the fruit of the Spirit in Galatians 5:22–23 (NLT).

"But the fruit of the Spirit is love, joy, peace, patience, kindness, goodness, faithfulness, gentleness, self-control; against such things there is no law."

Listening is not just the auditory voice outside of us but rather the awareness of God's presence. In His presence we feel His heart, see visions like a daydream, have thoughts we had not thought about before. Listening allows us to hear God from the inside where our spirit and His Spirit commune.

For the practice of prayer and listening, it is necessary to know the truth of who God is. There are so many titles given to God in the Bible and each one reveals something true about Him. This truth helps us see Him rightly and then we can begin to build a relationship with the Lord in this way by letting Him into the areas of our life that need to experience Him. When we cannot understand the reality of one of these names as an experience in our own lives, then we have an invitation to find out why He is known in this way. The knowledge of God directly impacts how we pray.

Remember this time spent with the Lord is finding your seat beside Him where you can feel yourself become humble and then acknowledging who God is before we ever ask for anything. Speaking aloud or internally doesn't really matter but it does relate somewhat to body language and our ability to discern His presence with us. Declaring who He is, is like opening a door to the One who knocks so that He can come in as mentioned in Revelation, chapter 3, verse 20.

As we look at the Lord rightly, we are agreeing with who He says He is, and this alignment brings heaven and earth together wherever we are. In our declarations, we must listen to each declaration and focus on the fruit of His Spirit making the Lord known to us. We can actually identify Him and something happens to us; we begin to feel His strength, power, wisdom, and truth fill us along with the attributes of His Spirit. This union that happens in prayer allows us to know God and to learn His ways. As you take in His identity, His presence will increase in and around you. God will begin showing up in your prayer time. Your heart will focus on Him. However, be aware that your flesh will want to focus on you and your needs. You will have to resist making prayer about you. If you feel that one of these names of God is foreign to you, it is time to ask Him about this particular name and to reveal this part of Himself to you. It is time to study the Bible and to see Him for who He is.

"Building a fire" is really my way of saying you can slowly begin to enter into His presence by just saying who God is. Praises and adoration allow us to align with Him, and in this alignment, we become conscious of Him. Our innermost being interacting with the Holy Spirit makes room for revelation and understanding. We are transformed by this kind of prayer. In the midst of the declarations we listen, meaning we pay attention to what we are thinking or feeling in the moment. We become aware of God.

In this chapter, I am going to explain some of the titles of God that help us get to know Him better. As you see Him rightly, you start to understand why Jesus tells His disciples to begin praying "hallowed be Your name." He is telling the disciples that all of our prayers should start with praises, recognition of the Father, adoration, and declaration. So, here we go. Let's take a brief look at some of the names we see in Scripture about Him.

Abba, the Aramaic word, means *father*. When Jesus taught the disciples the famous Lord's Prayer in Matthew 6, He began with Abba. This is significant because we understand that the first and probably most important name to address Him by is, indeed, Abba. The actual meaning is more than relational father; Jesus was calling Him Father out of intimacy, but He was actually saying "the One I obey." In English we would actually relate more to calling Him "sir" as the word embodies honoring a position as well as inferring obedience. When we call God "Abba," we are essentially saying, "Father, whom I obey." Paul writes to the Romans in chapter 8 verse 15 (ESV), "For you did not receive the spirit of slavery to fall back into fear, but you have received the Spirit of adoption as sons, by whom we cry, 'Abba! Father!'" Paul is telling the early church that we cry out to Him in obedience because of an intimate relationship and recognition of His authority rather than simply crying "Father, Father" as if it were just a name; we cry out from sonship, seeking obedience. Paul is saying that the Spirit we received wants to obey the Father. When I consider this name for the Lord, my heart is moved with love for Him. It could only be out of a heart of love that one would be willing to obey, honor, and recognize His holy position as Father. If we are looking for intimacy with God, then we must first understand that He has and has always been our Father, and it is our delight to honor Him with our obedience.

Adonai means *LORD*. Yes, *LORD* with all capitals. This name expands upon Abba. When we translate *Adonai* in English, it becomes *master*, but the original context and meaning of this name is more than master, more than father. Adonai is one word that actually sums up three concepts of God. The first use of this name is in Genesis 15:2, where Abraham addresses God as Adonai Yahweh. Abraham is calling Him powerful, master, and father. By adding *Yahweh* to *Adonai*, Abraham is saying that God who is powerful, who is the master, who I intimately know as father, is the one who brings into existence whatever exists. As we come to an understanding of Adonai, who is our Lord and Master, we enter into a place of prayer able to ask Him to bring into existence His perfect will and way. Lordship becomes His title. If we can accept that, we can begin to recognize that He is Lord, He is master, and therefore our lives are in His hands, but because He is our father, we can be assured that our lives will be cared for just as a father cares for his children.

Alpha and Omega, Beginning and End, comes from a verse in Revelation 22:13 (ESV), "I am the Alpha and the Omega, the first and the last, the beginning and the end." When we call God Alpha and Omega, we are summing up a simple concept that He is eternal. As Jesus proclaims this powerful statement, we understand that God is the eternal one. He is the author and the finisher of our faith as Hebrews 12:2 says and is the One who brings everything to pass. It is in the Alpha and the

Omega that we find God who fulfills the law so we can begin a new restored life through faith, not by works. The Eternal One, He has always been, and He will always be. As we enter into prayer, we can declare His eternal existence and recognize that in Christ Jesus, our life is headed for eternity. Hope arises, and we can see the temporary life we are now living will pass away but eternity remains.

Christ, the Anointed One, is the Hebrew word for "the anointed one," referring to the Messiah that was prophesied in the Old Testament. The first mention of the Anointed One is in Genesis 3:15 when God promised to send the seed of the woman to destroy sin. *Jesus* is the name Gabriel told Mary to give to her baby, but *Christ* is the title He holds. When Scripture puts these together we see that Jesus, savior, is the chosen and anointed Messiah, and so His title is added to His name. The Savior Anointed One becomes the identification of Jesus Christ. Peter understands this when he answers the question from Jesus in Matthew 16:16 (ESV), "You are the Christ, the son of the living God." As we pray in this way, we allow Jesus, who holds this title of Savior Anointed One to invade our lives. We allow the Anointed One to anoint us to do the work that He did.

Among Jewish words, the *EL* that precedes so many other descriptions of God is simply the word for *God*, denoting power, strength, and almightiness. As we discover more about who God is, we have some names that tell us exactly what God is like. His character and nature are revealed to us. As we look at the El names of God, consider your prayers of adoration that become full of the powerful holiness that is God.

El Deah: God of Knowledge. God is all knowing. There is nothing He needs to learn because God knows everything that was, is, and is to come. There are no surprises for Him and all knowledge is in Him. He completely encompasses everything that can be learned. We find *El Deah* in Exodus 15:2; Numbers 23:22; Deuteronomy 7:9; and Mark 15:34. All of these passages are used to describe the characteristic of God as the one who is all knowing. He knows the past, the present, and the future.

El Elyon: The God Most High, is a phrase used in Genesis 14 when describing Melchizedek as "priest of God Most High" (verse 18, ESV). Later in Hebrews, Jesus is given recognition as "priest forever, after the order of Melchizedek" (Hebrews 7:17, ESV). All this means that Jesus would be high priest forever whereas Melchizedek was only temporarily priest. However, the connection between them infers that *El Elyon* is Lord of Lords, King of Kings, God of all gods. He is the highest and there is no other greater than Him. So when we pray focusing on *El Elyon*, we are lifting Him up as the highest, the greatest, that there is no other above Him.

El Roi: The God who Sees Me, is the name in which we are introduced to God through Hagar. She gives this name to God as she is sitting in the desert thinking that she would surely die. At this moment, Hagar understood that God knew her heart, her feelings, and He could relate to her situation. God's ability to see us is to know us better than anyone else. Jesus would reiterate in the New Testament as He would often know the thoughts of those around Him, proving that He knew them. In Matthew 22:18 we see an example of the Pharisees trying to trick Jesus by asking Him a question that they believe will get Him in trouble. But verse 18 (NIV) says, "But Jesus, knowing their evil intent, said, 'You hypocrites, why are you trying to trap me?'" Jesus is aware of who they really are and the motives of their heart. He sees them for who they really are. In John 4, we see a similar story as Jesus is at a well and a Samaritan woman comes to get water. Jesus begins to talk to her; He reveals that He knows who she is, how many times she's been married, and that the man she is currently with is not her husband. He is revealing to her that He sees her, and He knows her. When we are praying to the Lord, aware that He sees us, we can come to Him with an honest heart because we know He sees us. We can enter into His presence without shame because our God sees us and our situation. He knows our problems, and He knows our successes.

El Shaddai: God Almighty, is the name by which Abraham calls the Lord when he has been promised many descendants. His recognition of God's ability to do the impossible is embodied in the words *El Shaddai*, who is God of the impossible. It is the name that reveals His power, able to do impossible things in the midst of our trials. It is *El Shaddai* that allows the kind of testing that empties us of ourselves. As we come in prayer to *El Shaddai*, we can be assured that He is able to do impossible things in our lives. We bring to Him the most impossible with full hope that He, our Lord, will make a way to do what seems completely outside of our ability or our situation.

Elohim: The Almighty Creator, is first used in Genesis 1:1 as we are introduced to the beginning of all that is created. Then Elohim said, "Let us make mankind in our image, in our likeness" (Genesis 1:26, NIV). His name, given here and in 2,000 other places in Scripture, alludes to the Trinity. However, *Elohim* is also used to express all other created beings such as angels, whether they're heavenly or fallen. This use would be the little *elohim* whereas the Almighty Creator is a capital *Elohim*. These little grammatical nuances allow hierarchy to be established. Seeing God as the Almighty Elohim means that everything we see and cannot see He made. He formed it; He shaped it; He called it into being from nothingness. When we are praying, it is to the only True God, who has created everything.

Yahweh: I Am, is the name that God Himself tells Moses in Exodus 6:2–3. This is His eternal name and would be the name He would be known as for generations to come. When He tells Moses to call Him *Yahweh*, He also explains it as *"I AM WHO I AM"* (Exodus 3:14, NIV). This gives us some context for understanding the name *Yahweh*. Essentially we are calling Him eternal as in *the one who exists on his own and all things exist because of him* (Colossians 1:16). John would explain this as well in the New Testament when describing Jesus, John 1:2–3 (NIV), "He was with God in the beginning. Through him all things were made, and without him nothing was made that has been made." I often think as I am praying and considering Yahweh, that He was in all of history, and He will be in all of the future because He has always been, and He always will be. He is the uncreated one; He is eternal. When we understand this, then we can understand why Jesus says to Philip, "Anyone who has seen me has seen the Father" (John 14:9, NIV). Jesus is revealing to Philip that He was with the Father at the beginning and so He, too, has always existed.

Yahweh Nissi: The LORD My Banner, is in Isaiah 11:10 (NIV) where it says that "the root of Jesse [Jesus] will stand as a banner for the peoples." This is a prophesied promise for Israel who will defeat their enemies. God is speaking to His people about their battles. He is establishing that their battles are His battles, and He enables them to defeat their enemies. And as all winning sides do, the banner of victory is hung for all to see. Jesus became the banner of victory. He hung on a cross. There are times when we are praying and the only position we can hold is that Jesus is victorious, and we must wave that banner high, giving all praise to the One who wins our battles.

Yahweh Rapha: The LORD that Heals, is introduced to us in Exodus 15. It is in this story that we first get a glimpse at the God who heals. It happens when God's people are in a desert; they are in the midst of a tremendous difficulty. The only water to drink is salty and bitter. Sometimes in life, our situations may seem like a desert. We cannot escape the salty, bitter water that seems to be the only available drink. But God comes to change our situations. He is *Rapha* who heals, and in this story, we discover that God takes this undrinkable water and He gives us sweet water to drink. Later in John 7:37 (ESV), Jesus shouts to the crowds, "If anyone thirsts, let him come to me and drink." This is the One we pray to; He is the One who can take a bitter situation and make it sweet. Our God is the One that can take every bad thing and truly turn it around for our good.

Yahweh Shalom: The LORD is Peace. *Shalom* is the word for peace but not peace like the world. We first see this name in the book of Judges when Gideon builds an altar and names it Yahweh Shalom. Gideon understood peace as wholeness, harmony, and completeness. It is not based on circumstances but rather comes from the internal understanding that in every circumstance, we can be at peace. When Gideon came face-to-face with the Lord, he was afraid. But the angel of the Lord, most likely Jesus, said to him, "Peace to you. Do not fear; you shall not die" (Judges 6:23, ESV). It is inferred in this interaction that Gideon probably expected to die. Every Israelite would have known from the days of Moses, who asked to see the Lord, that no human can see God's face and live. However, Gideon discovers that the peace of God would, indeed, allow him to live. The revelation here is knowing that His glory is so massive that it could destroy us, but His peace is life-giving. These titles to His name reveal more facets of who God is as well as all that He embodies and can do. He is still massive in glory, but He is also the originator of peace, the one who brings wholeness, completeness, and harmony so that we do not die. Later the apostle Paul recounted His name while blessing the church in Thessalonica, "Now may the Lord of peace himself give you peace at all times in every way. The Lord be with you all!" (2 Thessalonians 3:16, ESV).

Yahweh Shammah: The LORD is There. In Ezekiel 48:35, we encounter the Lord in a heavenly vision of the coming kingdom. It is in this vision that Ezekiel sees that the city of God will be known for the presence of

God. He is there. This is significant because the understanding of His presence means life, and all that comes
abundantly is found in His presence; in His city. Where
the Lord is, there is blessing, protection, healing, wholeness, and life. Throughout the story of God, we see the
impact of His being there. The burning bush, inflamed
by God's presence, calls Moses to destiny and yet the
bush is not destroyed. We immediately realize that the
Lord who knows the plans He has for us, won't destroy
us in the midst of the plans. We see the deliverance mes-
sage come alive in a people let out of slavery, through
the waters and deserts that would otherwise destroy
them and into a Promised Land. God who is with them
comes as a cloud by day and a fire by night. The cloud
of shade to protect and fire to keep them warm. He is
the provider and the protector and the deliverer. Where
God is, there is abundance and life. The Lord's presence
in Obed-Edom's household brought blessings and the
news of his blessings spread, causing King David to go
retrieve the Ark of the Covenant. Where God is, there is
life. So, Ezekiel sees the coming city where life is eternal, and the Lord says it is because He is there. How
amazing it is to know that our God never leaves us nor
forsakes us and it is Him, Emmanuel, that is with us.

 Yahweh Tsabbaoth: The LORD of Hosts. King David
called out Goliath who defied the Lord of Hosts with
his taunting and threats. It is in 1 Samuel 17:45 (ESV)

that we hear this glorifying title given to the Lord. It encompasses the understanding that God has all power and is above all other authorities. He has the final and complete authority over everything. The Lord of Hosts means His army and all resources are at His will. Elisha understood this characteristic of the Lord as he asked for his servant's eyes to be open to see the Lord's army. His servant, in 2 Kings 6 is afraid of King Aram's army that is surrounding the city, but then his eyes are opened and there before him on the mountain was an army of horses and chariots of fire. They were, indeed, surrounding King Aram's army in such great numbers that victory was just on the horizon. God has all power, all resources at His command. There is nothing that can come against His plans. He always defeats His enemies.

Yahweh Tsidkenu: The LORD Our Righteousness. We all understand that God is righteous. He is, after all, sinless and perfect. This amazing attribute is mentioned in Jeremiah as a promise. In chapter 23, Jeremiah begins to prophesy to the nation of a righteous branch that will come to bring restoration. He is, of course, speaking of Jesus Christ. It comes as hope in a time where everything seems to be destroyed. The whole nation is entering exile to Babylon. God promises to restore which means His people will be made righteous because He is righteous. Full restoration looks like a people who live in righteousness. Jesus, our Savior, brings about restoration by making us right with God. We live in accordance with His ways, and we align our every decision with His wisdom. It is only because of Him that we are able to be made clean and undefiled. Salvation and righteousness cannot be separated. They come as a promise in His kingdom.

Yahweh Jireh: The LORD will Provide. In Genesis 22 we read of Abraham going to Mount Moriah to sacrifice his son Isaac. It is the revelation of God, the provider, breaking forth in the intense moment when doubt or hopelessness could have easily slipped in. Abraham tells Isaac that God will provide the sacrifice and indeed He does. Abraham sees the ram caught in the thicket and knows that God will provide the sacrifice. God will provide. Why? The Hebrew word *Yireh* means "to provide" as well as "to see." This is significant because God who sees, knows what we need and He provides. In this event in Abraham's life, God reveals that He sees the need for a sacrifice and He alone will provide what is needed. Abraham knows at this moment that Isaac is not what is needed but Jesus is the perfect sacrifice. God knows exactly what is needed. He is the provider.

All of these attributes of the Lord are intended to show us more and more of who He is. As we begin to see Him and trust Him, it develops intimacy and relationship with God. This changes our prayers because we begin to pray out of who He is and not from who we are. It is important to meditate on these names and titles. Consider who God is in relationship to us and begin offering to Him praise for the titles given to Him. It is important that the discipline of prayer be first addressed in the identity of God and why we spend time worshiping Him. As we take time to adore the Lord, we discover that our hearts, soul, mind, body, and strength begin to love Him completely. You may even, as you pray, begin to sense His Holy Spirit in physical ways such as warmth, unusual peace, shaking, or boldness, faith, joy, or other attributes of the Lord. The fruit of His Spirit begins to be felt in us.

Enter Your Gates with Thanksgiving (Psalm 100:4)

In Psalm 100, we are given these keys to a deeper prayer life which overflow into our relationship with God. This particular Psalm reveals actual steps to interacting with God. It is a short Psalm where every verse is a key to intimacy with Him. I want us to look at verse 4 where we are told to enter with thanksgiving. It is through prayers of thankfulness that we can get past our circumstances and enter into a reality beyond our own. Thankfulness seems easy, but the truth is, most people struggling cannot find something to be thankful for. It takes a revelation from the Lord to see blessings. It takes understanding the cost He paid for us to live free. This revelation leads one to call on the name of the Lord. Though our Western culture lumps all spiritual communication into prayer, it is important to understand that thankful "prayer" really is closer to a phrase in the Old Testament, "calling on the name of the Lord." This phrase implies worship and offerings. Even more so, it implies that God who is with us is beside us in everything we do. To grasp this fully is to understand that we are able to communicate with God because we are present with Him. Though this is a form of prayer to you and me, it is different from intercession, which we will discuss later. We want to be careful in mundane and busy lives that we do not get so used to God's provision, protection, and help that we forget to thank Him. It can become easy for us to take Him and our relationship for granted. Such lack of gratitude can rob Him of the glory due to Him. We can be oblivious to the help of the Lord when we start to feel like we are able to meet our own needs, protect, or provide for ourselves. This hinders the prayers of believers. A lack of thanksgiving and acknowledgement of the Lord's part has been forgotten and suddenly the believer's prayer lacks power. You may know from personal experience, or I am sure you have heard from others, how their prayer lives are lacking until they are in difficult places and seasons. I would not desire for anyone to learn about need from lack. It is a difficult lesson but rather one that seems to be required among many. I am sure that all people, at some time or another, find themselves in need. Nevertheless, this becomes an opportunity for God to reveal Himself. It would be much better if we could all learn that God "makes his sun rise on the evil and on the good, and sends rain on the just and on the unjust" (Matthew 5:45, ESV). Such a revelation allows our blessings to be acknowledged as a gift from Him. Our prayers come from humility, offering our gratitude. If we lose sight that He is the provider, protector, and helper, we cannot enter His gates because we have no way of relating to Him. As mentioned earlier, we pray to God based on how we know Him.

His Name, Not Our Name

Genesis 11:4 (ESV), *"Let us make a name for ourselves."*

In the book of Genesis, we have many accounts of the history of mankind, good and bad, but one in particular is the story of the Tower of Babel. In this account, we see that mankind has developed into a civilization that doesn't seek the help of God but rather seeks to make a name for themselves. They are building a monument of greatness and taking all the glory for themselves. Their intention is to be recognized by their own efforts. The Lord intervenes in this in an effort to keep them from being consumed by pride. All this occurred after the flood, after the Lord had sent them forth to spread out over the earth. Nimrod, the main figure in the building of this tower, was considered the first mighty man after the flood (Genesis 10:8). He obviously was ungrateful for his successes and was after acknowledging his own mightiness. So often our own successes keep us from grateful lives. He is someone who had decided to call upon his own name.

Nimrod was stealing all glory from God and had decided his tower would be for his own name. He wanted all the power, glory, and recognition for himself. He was not interested in calling on the name of the Lord or aligning himself with God. In fact, the whole disbursement of Nimrod and the people, by confusing their language so they could not communicate, was to protect them from the harm they would do with attitudes of self-promotion, pride, and ambitions of becoming renown. God was for them even in their rebellion of Him. He would, as we know, restore language in Acts 2 when the Spirit came and they spoke in tongues. All was designed to bring unity back to people as the disciples could now bring glory to God as the Jews in the city understood what they were saying in their own languages.

This is the power of glory given to God and gratitude for all He does to bring us to transformation as we become a new creation. Developing a life of thanksgiving is formative to our relationship with Him. We are constantly offering praise and glory for all that God does. It is a reflection of who He is and how dependent we are on Him. Nimrod could not be thankful as he had no praise to offer. He was not interested in building for God but rather for himself. Thankfulness is necessary to maintaining humility and keeping the focus on the One who can do all things.

Realizing our need for God produces thankfulness. They go hand in hand like the balancing of scales. We offer our thankfulness to God with every need we have, causing a mysterious balance in life to manifest, where increase comes and lack diminishes. Knowing God and calling on Him become the waves of relationship in our everyday lives. It is the communication, known as prayer, upon waking up and laying down at night that we are drawn deeper into a relationship with our Lord.

The practice of calling on Him, thanking Him, praising Him, and building that fire as we acknowledge God, above all, is where listening to Him begins. Prayer is part us and part Holy Spirit. We pray short prayers of adoration and thanksgiving and then we listen. In the listening, we begin to interact with God by His Spirit, and in this place, we gain wisdom, understanding, and revelation as it may pertain to Him or to us. This kind of relationship is the catalyst for transformation. A person is changed in the presence of God. A person is able to adjust and make new decisions when new information is available. We cannot break a lie unless we know it is a lie. We cannot see how God is using everything in our lives unless He shows us. Listening is allowing your whole body, being, to enter into a greater reality where things start to make sense. During this practice of prayer, we listen. We speak in short phrases and pay attention to every thought and feeling, becoming aware of God who is with us. In the next chapter, we will look at how listening is not simply an auditory response but an all-encompassing action of the mind, the body, and the spirit.

CHAPTER SIX

Seeing, Hearing, Knowing

*"When the Spirit of truth comes, he will guide you
into all the truth, for he will not speak on his own
authority, but whatever he hears he will speak, and
he will declare to you the things that are to come."*
John 16:13 (ESV)

The voice of the Lord draws us into the plans of His heart, and in this place, we find a way to partner with what God is saying to us about our own lives, the lives of others, and the plans He has for all mankind. Our ability to listen allows us to enter "into the Spirit" as the New Testament recounts and implores. To be in the Spirit is to be motivated and led by the Holy Spirit to do or to know the will of God. It is to act as the Holy Spirit leads. It is our ability to receive direction from the Lord so that we can partner with God's divine will. Ultimately it means we are of the same mind and willing to do as He would do.

The will of the Father is where unity in prayer exists. The Holy Spirit teaches us the will of God. By praying back to God what the Spirit says to us, we are partnering with His will. My heart and His heart begin to align and agreement comes, bringing heaven and earth together.

In Ezekiel 37, we see a great example of the partnership between heaven and earth when we are in the Spirit. This is a very common story that most of us know well, but I am going to emphasize the back and forth between Ezekiel and the Lord.

> Ezekiel 37:1 (ESV), *"The hand of the* LORD *was upon me, and he brought me out* **in the Spirit** *of the* LORD *and set me down in the middle of the valley; it was full of bones."*

The story begins with Ezekiel in the Spirit, being led by the Spirit to a valley full of bones. It is clear that Ezekiel is seeing this with his eyes in the Spirit. Seeing in the Spirit is when we start to see pictures or a movie-like story play out in our minds. It could also be a picture or a movie right in front of us with our natural eyes. This is one way the Holy Spirit shows us what the Father is saying. It could also be like a daydream or a still photo.

I remember when I first started seeing pictures pop into my mind while I was praying. I felt like I was being distracted and I kept trying to ignore these thoughts. Then I realized the Holy Spirit was trying to tell me what was on the Father's heart. I was reminded of Proverbs 15:3 (ESV) where Scripture tells us that "the eyes of the LORD are in every place, keeping watch on the evil and the good." I would see faces of people I did not know and soon I realized how the Father sees everyone and how they are in His sight. I could see His heart for them. So, with this vague impression, I began to thank God that He loves all the people and that He sees them. It was in this simple acknowledgement that I felt His compassion rise up and His boldness to ask for them to know Him more. This is the beginning of partnering with God in prayer. I was entering into a place of asking God to do what God wanted to do.

Ezekiel did the same. In verse 4, we see that the Spirit of the Lord told him to prophesy to the bones. *4 (ESV):* "*Then he said to me, 'Prophesy over these bones, and say to them, O dry bones, hear the word of the LORD.'*"

Then it happened and Ezekiel does as the Spirit leads him. *7 (ESV):* "*So I prophesied as I was commanded. And as I prophesied, there was a sound, and behold, a rattling, and the bones came together, bone to its bone.*"

When we are in the Spirit or of the same mind, we can see what the Father is doing and how He thinks. The Holy Spirit will tell us what to pray, and in this particular story, we can see that Ezekiel was prophesying, which is one way we know how to pray the will of God.

Let's look at another example of seeing in the Spirit. In Acts 10:9–16 we see that Peter goes up on the roof to pray. While food is being prepared, and Peter is hungry, he falls into a trance. A trance is a lot like a daydream. You may not be aware of your natural surroundings, but you are fully aware of the daydream. In this trance, Peter sees heaven open up and a large sheet let down. He sees all of these animals that he would not eat as a Jewish man, but verse 13 (NIV) says, "Then a voice told him, 'Get up, Peter. Kill and eat.'" As we read on, we see that Peter is unsure of the vision and he argues with the voice. Then in verse 16 (NIV), it says, "This happened three times, and immediately the sheet was taken back to heaven." Peter does wake up and as many of us would do, we begin to think about what we just saw. We call it processing. Now Peter gets his answer almost immediately as Cornelius sends servants to collect Peter and this is the beginning of a Jewish man ministering to a non-Jew and his family. Sometimes, we get pictures, visions, dreams and we need to process what God is telling us. For us the answer may come immediately or over time. Regardless, the vision is a way of seeing what the Father wants to do and then we can partner with Him. In this story of Peter's prayer time, we see that Peter gains understanding about what is clean. If it were not for this vision in prayer, Peter would not have seen Cornelius and his family as clean. He would not have seen them the way God does.

When we are drawing close to the Lord, it is essential that we develop agreement with how He sees people, the world, and us. God is so beautiful in the way He patiently speaks to us. Every believer who is trying to not be distracted by thoughts in their mind, which usually come passing by, might be missing the opportunity to see problems, people, and life the way God does. We get invited into moments where all we can do is ask, like Peter: What does this mean? God uses the Word to help us process and to help us understand if this is His heart that we are seeing or if it is our own. It takes an intimate relationship to know the difference between our thoughts and His. Over time, we see what He sees. Jesus would tell us in John 5 that the Son can only do what He sees His Father doing. How incredibly profound is that statement. If we learn to see what the Father is doing, we can pray in agreement and do what He is doing. When we can see that God loves someone or hates something deceptive, we know how we also will respond. This is intercession. This is prayer. This is a relationship with the Almighty God and Savior of the world.

Hearing

Hearing is another way we can receive the Father's heart, but we need to be in the Spirit or of a sound mind. As Paul told Timothy in 2 Timothy 1:7 (ESV), "For

God gave us a spirit not of fear but of power and love and self-control."

Prayer helps us to be in the right frame of mind and heart so that we can hear the Lord. The Lord speaks to us in whispers, impressions, spontaneous thoughts, and even audibly if necessary.

John, on the island of Patmos, says he was "in the Spirit on the Lord's day, and I heard behind me a loud voice like a trumpet" (Revelation 1:10, ESV). John hears the voice of the Lord and begins to see and hear what the Lord has to share about the churches, the coming events on the earth, and most of all, he is discovering the kingship of Jesus Christ. Prayer takes us into the heart of the Father, and in this place, the Holy Spirit tells us things we could not have known before.

When I was around seventeen years old, I was sitting in my bedroom on the floor, singing and folding socks. When suddenly I heard a loud voice that seemed to shake me, saying "You're going on a mission trip." I froze and felt like this voice, so loud, shook me and before I even processed it, I said, "No, I'm not!" Then it hit me. I had just heard the Lord. This would not leave me for several days, and I began to feel uneasy about it. But one night before sleeping, as I prayed, I decided it must have been the Lord telling me to go on a mission trip, so I prayed in agreement and told Him that I would go wherever He wanted me to. The following Sunday at church, for the first time, our pastor announced that our church would be doing the very first mission trip. I was stunned, but I was also certain that I was supposed to be on that first mission trip.

Hearing is essential to our walk with God, and it is the job of the Holy Spirit to tell us these things. We need to be prepared and allow our spiritual ears to hear what the Father is saying.

Isaiah explains hearing as he is prophesying the Word of the Lord. Isaiah 30:21 (ESV) says, *"And your ears shall hear a word behind you, saying, 'This is the way, walk in it,' when you turn to the right or when you turn to the left."* Hearing is the sound of the Lord giving us direction, helping us make decisions, and watching over our path. When we can receive His direction, we make good decisions, and our path is made straight. The primary measuring stick to hearing God is to be able to discern if what we think we hear is indeed Him. Some believers have itchy ears, which 2 Timothy speaks about in regard to people not having sound doctrine and lusting after their own desires. When this is in the heart of a believer, they can be sure to hear only what they want to hear. It is why everything we hear needs to align with the Word of God and reflect who He is just as we talked about in earlier chapters. God's character and His promises are eternal, so everything we hear must consistently align with who He is and what He has promised. We cannot use Scripture out of context just so we justify our itchy ears. Hearing is about knowing the heart and will of God and being able to understand how what we hear aligns with the Bible. The Holy Spirit inspired the writing of Scripture, and the Holy Spirit speaks to us the will of God. These two must be in alignment and used as a measuring stick for our hearing. I think we can find some guidelines in Scripture to help us discern our hearing God versus itchy ear syndrome.

John 3:16, which is probably one of the most well-known verses, tells us how much God loved the world. When we hear in the Spirit, love must be in the tone and words. God loves even in discipline which Hebrews 12 tells that all discipline is the result of His love. When God is speaking to us, even in correction, there really is no condemnation. His correction feels loving and this can give us certainty that we are most likely hearing His voice over the hateful, condemning, judgmental, and accusatory voice of the enemy. I am not saying God doesn't warn us or tell us to guard our hearts because He does indeed. However, that leads to my next point on hearing God. He will protect us. His Word and His character support this absolute truth: God is our protector. When we hear a warning or discern that something or someone is not safe, we are again most likely hearing God, our protector. He will guide us in paths of safety because God tells us that He will advise us so our life is safe. So often we do not listen to these warnings from the Holy Spirit, and we find ourselves in retrospect realizing we knew in our hearts to not pursue something or someone and yet we did. But this actually helps us understand that hearing God means God speaks what is good, pure, and holy. If what we hear aligns with sin or harm, we are not hearing God. God does not bless sin or hatred. God would not speak to us in any way that would encourage us to give into sin or hatred. When He speaks, it is to bring life and to produce a future that is good, pure, and holy. However, I would say that God, who calls us to repentance, does speak about sin when it is to bring us to repentance. This is where love and compassion are most felt. If God speaks to us about sin in a person, ourselves, or our nations, it is to bring it all to repentance. He does not ask us to call fire down on people. When the disciples in Luke 9 wanted to call down fire on people, Jesus rebukes them and says, "You do not know what manner of spirit you are of" (verse 55, NKJV). He is making it clear that this thought did not come from the Father. However, we also see in Matthew 16, when Peter is asked, "But who do you say that I am?" (verse 15, NKJV) that Jesus responds by confirming that man could not have told Peter this, but the Father showed Peter this truth.

All this to say, hearing God is about truth. It is about the Holy Spirit telling us truth that breaks lies and brings revelation so that we can see rightly, and we can speak in truth because we hear what the Father is saying. Even in the Old Testament, people understood that God only speaks truth. He does not lie so there can be no contradiction from His Word and what we hear.

Knowing

When the Holy Spirit speaks in words or pictures, great revelation may seem like a lot of information coming all at once. This is what I would call knowing. For many people, a knowing experience is a combination of vision and hearing. It comes with more understanding though not much was seen or heard. Knowing is like seeing the face of someone you know well and without words, you know what they are thinking. It is like a loved one saying a short phrase, but you know what they really mean.

Some people compare it to a download, meaning they had a brief moment in the prayer where a much bigger idea, concept, or knowledge was given to them. It is information they heard or saw but has more meaning than the actual phrase, words, or pictures. The Holy Spirit teaches us the truth and gives us wisdom and knowledge, helping us align with the will of God. Paul explains this to the Corinthians in 1 Corinthians 2:9–11 (ESV).

But, as it is written, "What no eye has seen, nor ear heard, nor the heart of man imagined, what God has prepared for those who love him"—these things God has revealed to us through the Spirit. For the Spirit searches everything, even the depths of God. For who knows a person's thoughts except the spirit of that person, which is in him? So also no one comprehends the thoughts of God except the Spirit of God.

Paul is telling them that all things are revealed through the Holy Spirit, and we could not know the Father's mind unless the Holy Spirit tells us. This is knowing Him. When we pray and the Spirit reveals the mind of Christ, we begin to understand the perspective of heaven. We gain understanding of His ways and His thoughts towards us and how He plans to bring all things unto Himself. We can take this wisdom and knowledge and begin to pray in agreement, telling the Lord we want what He wants. After all, how can a person be heard in heaven? How can God hear us? We need to be in agreement with Him and two things will most certainly happen. We will be heard, and we will see our requests are answered. Knowing the heart of God is praying according to His thoughts and desires. And, as John expressed, *"And this is the confidence that we have toward him, that if we ask anything according to his will he hears us. And if we know that he hears us in whatever we ask, we know that we have the requests that we have asked of him"* (1 John 5:14–15, ESV).

Ultimately, knowing God is our ability to understand His character and ways. If we were to study all the parables, Old Testament and New, we would learn about God's kingdom versus man's kingdom. We would get to know how God sees the world He made and how He wants it to properly function. It is in the study of the Bible that we learn the way God sees, thinks, and moves. In our prayers, we start to hear and see the truth of Scripture come to us in more personal parables as well as words of knowledge or wisdom. The Holy Spirit, who is perfectly aligned with the Son and Father, begins to teach us personally about the character and movements of God without ever breaking unity and consistency with the Word of God. To know Him is to truly be a friend who can rightly administer His plans and understand His ways. We have authority to influence through prayer to create a world that He desires.

When we begin to know God, we gain understanding. This comes to us as words of knowledge and words of wisdom. These work together by the Holy Spirit to first identify the problem or situation, which is the word of knowledge. How can we know the root of a problem when we do not know all the details of the world's problems? But God does. He knows the thoughts, motives, private conversations, and the unseen entities that are in the heavenlies. Until He gives us knowledge, we can only see what we currently understand. Then God, who sees everything, tells us. Even then we only see in part as 1 Corinthians 8:2 (ESV) tells us, "If anyone imagines that he knows something, he does not yet know as he ought to know." However, the word of wisdom, which Solomon so rightly valued, allows us to see and know the solution to the problems.

Gideon would not have imagined that a smaller army would be the solution to winning a battle and yet the solution was not a bigger army but rather a specific few. For God was telling Gideon the real problem is the arrogance of men who think their own hands could save them. In our natural understanding, we would logically think the problem was Midian and the solution would be a bigger army. But to God, the problem was pride and arrogance among His people and the solution was a smaller army. Prayer allows us to understand how God sees the problem and the solution.

Many of us have been pushing visions, pictures, daydreams, and thoughts away, trying to focus and pray, but it is possible that God is trying to tell you something. We need to pay attention to the things we see, hear, and know when we are listening during prayer.

Once our hearts and thoughts are on Him and we are not approaching God with lots of words and wish lists, then we can begin to pray for all things to be on earth as it is in heaven. God wants to talk to us about His ways, His thoughts, and His plans. In fact, we need to remember Amos tells us in chapter 3:7 (NIV), "Surely the Sovereign LORD does nothing without revealing his plan to his servants the prophets." This is remarkable. God wants to tell His people His plans. We only need to practice listening when we are praying.

CHAPTER SEVEN

The Word Confirms

Words do indeed have power and they are felt when spoken. As a parent, I can recall the power of my words when speaking to my children. My daughter, who felt she knew my heart, at a young age would come to tell me what her brothers were doing and why it was wrong. As I would respond to her saying, "Tell them I am coming and will take care of it." She could be heard saying, "Mom says she is going to spank you." Our words mean something. As amused as I was at her translation of my words, the sentiment was that discipline is coming. When our Father in heaven speaks, we too understand the sentiment and may often translate His words for others to receive. However, the Word of God is written so that all of us can receive it with the help of the Holy Spirit. It is good for us to read His Word, know the context, and apply it appropriately. When something does not align with the written word, we have every right to question it. Whether God is disciplining those He loves or calling them into a deeper relationship, we need to know that what we see, hear, feel, or think aligns with His words.

> Matthew 4:4 (NIV), *"Jesus answered, 'It is written: "Man shall not live on bread alone, but on every word that comes from the mouth of God."'"*

Though tempted, Jesus understood that all life comes from the words of God and life is not in the desires of the flesh. Afterall, Jesus is the Word of God made flesh. He is the *logos* word, meaning that Jesus is the spoken Word of God from the beginning in Genesis to the end of Revelation. He is the fulfillment of God's words.

> *"In the beginning was the Word, and the Word was with God, and the Word was God"* (John 1:1, NIV).

God's Word is creative, and when creative words come out of our mouths, we can create life or even death (Proverbs 18:21). Our words have power and when spoken, they eventually manifest. Proverbs 13:2 says that our words produce fruit. It is reiterated in Matthew 12:36–37, as we understand that our words will either acquit or condemn us. We all give an account for the careless words we speak. The weighty responsibility of our words is sobering but manageable. We choose words. We choose how we speak and when we speak. Does it take discipline? Sure. It is a practiced, intentional, and conscious decision to produce life. However, it takes the work of the Holy Spirit to remind us and to illuminate the Word so that we see just how God divides it all up and separates us from the world.

The Holy Spirit who was sent to teach us truth, who has come to help us pray, is also the One who will help us speak life. It is the heart and will of God to use our words to encourage, to build up, and to call it as though it were. How often do we use our words to vent or to tear down? We criticize and complain rather than speak as He would. We need to know His words and how He speaks. The image of the Lord, who is holy, is made clearer when we sound like Him. He becomes manifest, felt, and closer when the Word is spoken from His heart rather than our own.

It is our logical thinking that gets in the way of speaking as if He were speaking. We rationalize, we project, we judge, and all of it limits us, causing us to pray our way. We think our own way and speak our own way. But if we know how He is thinking, then we can speak His way. After all, we know that His ways are not our ways and His thinking is not our thinking (Isaiah 55:8).

When studying the Bible and searching for the depth of who God is—why He is doing what we read—we find deep love and righteousness. We begin to understand that God is not angry and violent or mad at anyone but rather He is the defender, just and loving. Only surface reading of the Bible gives us assumptions of God and His ways, but prayerful reading and studying results in the understanding of His marvelous ways.

How well do you know His character? How well do you know what He would do in any situation? We can literally spend a lifetime learning about Him and His ways. All of this forms and shapes our speech, and our words become His words that create and bring life. I believe with the help of the greatest helper, the Holy Spirit, we can grow into people who know how to use our words. We can talk like He talks. Being one that studies the Word is one that studies Jesus. Who knows Him better than the Holy Spirit? He will teach us to speak life, so that as we pray, we can pray for what God would desire and say.

> *"For the word of God is living and active, sharper than any two-edged sword, piercing to the division of soul and of spirit, of joints and of marrow, and discerning the thoughts and intentions of the heart"* (Hebrews 4:12, ESV).

Can you imagine the two-edged sword cutting through and piercing to the very core of who you are? It is a painful image and one that makes your eyes go wide. But the point is clear. When God speaks, His words go deep and the understanding that enlightens us is more than the words as it connects to experiences, senses, memories, and a future reality that leaves a revelation too great to ignore. It causes us to change. It causes us to transform, and in that transformation, we begin to know His ways.

We do not always understand the differences that exist in our lives. We cannot always understand the godly from the ungodly. But the Word of God does this for us. This sharp sword, translated from *machairan*, is more likely to be a dagger. Sharp enough to divide joints and marrow. For many of us, we don't see the difference but God does. It is His Word that helps us separate Him from the world.

"Sanctify them in the truth; your word is truth" (John 17:17, ESV).

What a beautiful word: sanctify! That our God would make us holy, set apart with His Word. Because His Word is the truth, we become consecrated and made legitimate children. His Word sanctified us, making us free from sin. This purity is given to us as we receive truth from His Word.

"Your word is a lamp to my feet and a light to my path" (Psalm 119:105, ESV).

For every one of us who has tried to walk around in the dark, we stumble, grab onto things, step on objects, and we stub those toes. Yet, if we had turned on the light, we could have avoided such tragedy. God's Word is the light that allows us to walk safely and to know where we are, as well as where we are going. As I ponder this verse, I am more aware that the Lord's character and will is revealed in this short, well-known verse. We see His concern for our safety as He turns on the light. We see that God is for our journey and He knows the path to take. His Word gives direction and it points the way to life everlasting.

> "So shall my word be that goes out from my mouth; it shall not return to me empty, but it shall accomplish that which I purpose, and it shall succeed in the thing for which I sent it" (Isaiah 55:11, ESV).

What assurance we have when we know that God spoke it. It is for certain that His Words accomplish and succeed. By knowing the Word of God, we can pull on His character, His promises, His faithfulness, and see it come to pass. When the Lord speaks, it is as good as done. I find this a place of rest, even when it is difficult to rest, because I can read His Word and speak it back to Him, not as one that accuses God but one that agrees with God. It is faith and hope on our part that are required, but His Words have power and creativity so that His purposes are fulfilled.

"So that faith comes from hearing, and hearing through the word of Christ" (Romans 10:17, ESV)

God's Word releases faith. Have you ever heard someone talk about doing something that you never thought about before? It is in these moments that we suddenly realize something else is possible. You may have even thought, *I didn't know I could do that!* We are people who need to hear the Word because it is life-giving and full of promises. But it is incredible to think that the Word of God produces faith for life and promise. It allows us to see a reality that we didn't know existed or was possible. Faith comes from hearing and faith is needed for the journey. When faith is produced, we can pray for, as well as aim for, the greater things Jesus said we would see and do.

"Heaven and earth will pass away, but my words will not pass away" (Matthew 24:35, ESV).

Eternity is in His Words. The words of our Lord remain in the good news that is preached, in the born-again person, in the creation itself as all the promises come colliding with each and every word that God spoke about eternity. Eternity is where everything is made right, and in righteousness, we enter into the fulfillment of His Words. Consider that all promises of God will come to pass and at some point, we will see the temporary pass over into eternal. Think about the voice of the One who is able to create when He speaks. He is making all things new, and He is the one that has the last words, words that are everlasting as words that define us, our world, and give us perspective beyond the smaller worlds we live in.

"Your words were found, and I ate them, and your words became to me a joy and the delight of my heart, for I am called by your name, O LORD, God of hosts" (Jeremiah 15:16, ESV).

Our mouths were made for words. We eat the Words given to us by God and these words taste so good. I like foods from so many different cultures. I enjoy tasting foods that I have never had before, and when I find something I enjoy the taste of, I just keep going back for more. God's Words are like this. They are made to fill up our mouths, be spoken, and bring joy and delight. His Words are words that make one's heart healthy. The more we become people who know His Word, the more we can speak it but only if it truly gets to the heart. It has to be consumed in order to touch the heart. The Word is not meant to be head knowledge. When we only know the Word as a memorized Word, it is like reading a recipe but never making the dish. In order to eat the words, we need to follow the recipe, make the dish, and consume it.

"The law of the LORD is perfect, reviving the soul"
(Psalm 19:7, ESV).

The law, in all its beauty, displays the heart of God for us and helps us to live for eternity, but Psalm 19 tells us that its perfection revives the soul. If you, like me, have had hard disappointments, grief, pain that sinks into your soul, then it is His beautiful Words written in the law that revive us. Life again is found in His perfect, unchanging law. We can count on it, and we can be certain that what God has said, He will do. This particular Psalm opens with the heavens declaring the glory of God. This comparison is one that helps us settle in our soul that each day is new, and God has put into motion this perfect law that will also go into effect over our world and our lives. Each day is a revived sense of who God is and that just as the sun makes its circuit each day, so will words of God.

"Death and life are in the power of the tongue, and those who love it will eat its fruits" (Proverbs 18:21, ESV).

Power is in the tongue. Words create, destroy, or produce fruit of some kind or another. We are indeed like the One who made us as we, too, can speak life or death. We may not have the final say on everything, but we do have power in our words. This power is meant to produce life and to destroy that which is evil. But ultimately, we are producing fruit. The way we speak about ourselves, others, and circumstances reveals everything about what we think and believe. These words need to be in agreement with God otherwise we may be agreeing with the way of the world or even worse, speaking like our enemy the devil. A disciplined tongue is important in the journey we take on with Jesus. It is our ability to speak accordingly and for His kingdom, not against it.

CHAPTER EIGHT

Processing the Heart of God

*"For the Spirit searches everything, even the depths
of God. For who knows a person's thoughts except
the spirit of that person, which is in him? So also
no one comprehends the thoughts of God except the
Spirit of God. Now we have received not the spirit of
the world, but the Spirit who is from God, that we
might understand the things freely given us by God."*
(1 Corinthians 2:10–12, ESV)

Because God speaks to us in pictures, short phrases,
and dreams, we need to be able to interpret what all of
it means. Sometimes we get a picture in our mind or
we just have a thought that passes. These little inter-
ruptions or what might even seem like distractions can
often be God talking to us. But without processing it,
we don't always know what He's saying. This is where
it's necessary to process all the information that is

coming to us in ways that it could be God. Many times, when I'm working with students, they will say they had a brief thought or a picture came to their mind. but they don't know what it means! When we know the Bible and there are Scriptures that are stored away in our hearts, we begin to develop wisdom. This wisdom gives us understanding and it is how we know the ways of God. As I have shared throughout this book, prayer isn't just the things that pop into your mind or passing thoughts or a dream in the night, but rather prayer is all of us, mind, body, soul, and spirit able to understand the heart of God the Father. As His Spirit, the Holy Spirit, lives within us, we can process the thoughts of God and the heart of God and the ways of God. I believe with everything in me this is how the Lord transforms us. He helps us see things from His perspective. He helps us understand His ways. It's all of this that helps us partner with heaven. We begin to pray or speak from His heart, His will, His ways.

In order to process the heart of God, we have to understand His character and His movements. All of the things that I've talked about in this book help us to understand His character. They help us to understand how He moves. It's keeping a record in our journals of what we see, what we hear, what we feel an impression of, and any verses or passages of the Bible that come to us. God has a way of giving us just enough to make us hungry and thirsty so that we go looking for more. A large part of your prayer time is taking what you saw, heard, felt within you as a knowing, and searching it out in the Word of God.

Think about those we read of in the Bible. Daniel had visions; Zechariah had visions, and so many other prophets had visions. Sometimes they asked the angel of the Lord, "What does this mean?" But other times, it's left for interpretation. All interpretation, even in the Bible, is interpreted by the Bible. The Bible is the most consistent source of who God is and the way He moves. So, when we are reading Scripture, we interpret it according to Scripture, and if it is a vision or a dream or just a deep knowing in your heart, it is best to interpret it according to Scripture. I know a lot of this is what we talked about in the last chapter; however, it is foundational to being able to process God's heart. When the Lord puts His heart in us, His eyes in us, and His ears in us, then we know that the Holy Spirit is trying to teach us truth.

I remember the story of a young woman who was recently married. She had had a very rough background and had grown up in rough circumstances, but when she came to the Lord, her heart, her life, and everything about her was so fully committed and freed from her past life. In this new marriage, she began to face challenges with her young husband in ways it tested her.

At first, when she came to me crying and upset, feeling like she was "doing everything," my heart went out to her and I felt sad for her. I began to pray for her. I could see and feel a strong knowing that God was in all of this. My prayer went something like this, "Lord, she has been through enough and this marriage should be one of joy and peace." Then I saw that God was cutting away these areas from her and in my heart, I knew they were all the remaining selfish parts. Even though my natural state wanted to see her life full of joy and peace with no problems, it was in prayer that I understood God was still transforming her, but this time she would be safe as He was the one helping her to let go of every selfish part of her flesh so that she could indeed live in marriage with joy and peace. Sometimes it is hard to trust God's process. We want to skip seasons that are hard, or we want to avoid the desert at all cost. But it is in the process that we begin to grow, change, and be transformed.

In the process of life, God will often take us through difficult seasons. This may feel like pruning or suffering. All suffering, all pruning is loss and that is painful. But just because it's painful, just because we go through it, doesn't mean that it isn't God's process. There are a few kinds of processes. There is a process of renewing your mind where we begin to think like God thinks. The Bible calls this the mind of Christ. There is a process of repentance where we see our sin, give it up, renounce it, and never return to it. There is a process of transition where you can't take it with you and so you lose everything. There is a process of building where patience is required while everything falls in place.

Trust the process is a common phrase used here at Global School of Supernatural Ministry because we know that every student who passes through this school is in some kind of process. However, they will come out of this school in a whole new season! Whatever process you may be facing, season by season, God is in it, and He is with you. Because I know that God is with us, in all seasons, I know He is for us and not against us. I can be certain that survival and success are before me as long as I keep my ears and my eyes and my heart and soul fixed on Him.

I had a dream once about the process. In the dream I was in a grocery store, and I was shopping for the best ingredients to make a perfect dish. While I was trying to pick out the perfect ingredients, I discovered that the best ingredients were down low, so I knelt below the stacked vegetables and reached down low to grab the best. In this part of the dream, I understood that in order to obtain the best in life, the best that God has for us, we have to go low. Low is a place of prayer. The dream went on, and as I stood up and looked at my shopping cart, I realized my wallet was open and everything had been taken out of it except for my ID. It was at this moment I knew that in order for me to reach for the best, I would lose it all; however, my identity would stay intact. The season that followed this dream was extremely difficult and I did indeed lose many things. I had to stay low, in prayer, and over time, I came out of that season with so much revelation, wisdom, faith, and power to overcome and to build a new life that was so much more aligned with His purposes. It took every day for me to trust the process and to know that God's heart was good and He had better plans for me than the plans I had for myself.

Let's think about King David. Before David was king, he was a shepherd boy. The prophet Samuel had picked David to be the next king of Israel, but David was just a boy. It would be years, many battles, and much rejection before David's life would be so completely transformed. It was then that he became king. Now we could say that David was king from the moment Samuel spoke it, but there was a process. David could not skip the process, otherwise he would not have become the king he was. When we consider this in our own lives, it may be like a dream, a word, a promise you've been carrying for a long time, which you may even think of giving up. But we have to remind ourselves that we are in a process. This process shapes us, refines us, and causes us to be fully transformed so that when that promise comes to pass, we are truly ready to step into it.

God has a plan and a purpose. His plan and His purposes come to pass because He always keeps His Word. If you and I allow Him to insert us into His plan and His purposes, it will cause us to walk through a process. In the end, we come out of it more aligned with Him, more in love with Him, and much more ready to set our hands to the task He's given us. As the Bible reminds us that we are to pray "on earth as it is in heaven" (Matthew 6:10, ESV), then it becomes necessary for us to be able to understand how heaven moves. How can anyone create on earth any kind of change that looks like heaven if you have not seen what heaven holds? We need a glimpse of the place that Jesus called paradise as He suffered on the cross. A glimmer of this place where rust, moths, and thieves cannot destroy it and it becomes a place we can create on earth. When we pray and process, we gain revelation of the place Jesus is preparing for us. Keep in mind that prayer is an intentional encounter with the supernatural so that we can understand how God thinks, who He is, and how His ways are different from our ways. If we can see it, if we can hear it, if we know it in our innermost being, then we can bring it to earth through our words, thoughts, and actions. It becomes reproducible, and in that reproduction, we change and become transformed. This is how we process the heart of God.

As we gain new understanding, we gain a vision of the way life can be and this fills us deep in our hearts and minds. Suddenly with our prayers, we can make new choices. We can choose to tear down strongholds that don't belong in our mind, and we can build up a refuge that is the mind of Christ. As we process, we look inward, and by looking at our own heart, we start to see what must change, who we need to forgive, who we release from unforgiveness in our own heart, and who we bless. When God gives us truth and understanding, by His Holy Spirit, it compels us to walk a process of change.

We can pray for the world around us to change, but it starts with our own heart. We can pray for family members to see the light and come out of darkness, but it starts with our own heart. We can pray for His kingdom to come and His will to be done, but we need a vision so that we understand what His kingdom looks like. It is only when we can behold what is on the other side of change, of process, of hope for a better world, for a healthier family and a kingdom that is everlasting, that it becomes an anchor that we hold on to until we see it manifest.

I think of a time I was praying for a situation where everything seemed ruined and destroyed. Truthfully, I was rather grieved and not completely sure if life would ever feel good again. But in my prayers the Lord showed me a picture. In this picture, I saw an old castle ruined and left abandoned, covered with overgrown trees, bushes, and jungle. I felt so sad the once big and beautiful castle was being swallowed by the forest around it. I started to pray that the Lord would restore the castle because I knew it was a picture of the life I felt like was ruined. Then I heard the Lord say in a small still voice, "You don't understand restoration." Suddenly there was a revelation that came, and I understood the original creation, the forest, the jungle was being restored. The castle was what man, me, had built. But God was restoring everything, and I was looking at the picture all wrong. Sometimes we need to process with the Holy Spirit to understand what God is doing and how we can pray for things the way He sees it. I repented for wanting to preserve my man-made life and started praying with agreement that God was the wiser one. I started praying He would help me live a new life that He had for me and that I would see things the way He sees them. It was humbling, and through my prayer life, partnered with Him, I began to live a whole new life with a whole new occupation, an opportunity that I would not have had if the castle remained.

Whatever the situation you are facing, prayer is the place to get perspective. God's perspective. Life is full of our own understanding and ways. But when we pray, we start to see things from God's perspective. It can be humbling and sometimes lead us to repentance, but how beautiful it is to see what the Lord will do if we lay down our man-made ways.

As you process your prayer time, there are some things to keep in mind. Biblical truth is absolute, and every situation must bow to the voice of the Lord, which is truth. When we pray, our understanding needs to be based on the truth. John 8:32 (ESV) says that "you will know the truth, and the truth will set you free." It is important that we remain as those abiding in Him so that we know the truth. A good comparison would be a plant with roots versus a cut flower. Abiding in Him allows us to stay free to live, but a cut plant has no roots and its life is limited. Truth is life-giving and has roots deep in the Lord.

Shadowboxing is another area to process or rather to avoid. Shadowboxing is when we are so motivated by fear, worry, anger, or some other strong emotion which causes us to pray like we are fighting. This is a scheme of the enemy to tire us out and to cause us to grow weary. We start praying like we are somehow going to "show him" who's boss. This is where the enemy uses our immaturity and emotions against us instead of resting in the truth of God and praying as He would. Let me give you an example. Jesus, after being baptized, went into the wilderness to be tempted by Satan. We read in the Gospels that He was tempted three times. If you notice how the Lord responded with truth each time, you will see that He did not allow Himself to get into some spiritual battle where He was fighting with Satan. But rather, Jesus responds with truth and stands on what is the Word of God. He defeats the temptations of the enemy and does not allow Himself to become more exhausted than His hungry, fasted body must have been. We often get into prayers that just wear us out and it is because we are fighting with an enemy that is just a shadow sent to bother us, to exhaust us. Standing on the truth, and with confidence in God, always produces effective prayers and these get answered.

Lastly, we need to consider our own motives; wrong motives become ideas and desires that we want, and this can affect how we pray. If we are seeking our will to be done, we will pray from a place of idols. All the things we long to glorify and gain for status, for comfort, for success become a driving force of our prayers. This affects our prayers and can also be exhausting. Wrong motives give us false vision and false hope. Ultimately, the enemy sets us up with our own desires and then disappoints us as we feel like God did not answer our prayers.

God is for us and not against us as Romans 8:31 reminds us. We need to stand on this truth and ask according to His will so that we live in the desire that He has for all of us. Even when we do not understand, we can be sure that God is working it all out for our good.

Our prayers become most effective when we can process how God sees our situation and begin to understand that His ways, though different, are the best ways.

Deeper Intimacy

*"And he said to him, 'You shall love the Lord your
God with all your heart and with all your soul and
with all your mind. This is the great and first commandment. And a second is like it: You shall love
your neighbor as yourself. On these two commandments depend all the Law and the Prophets.'"*
Matthew 22:36–40 (ESV)

Ultimately, our God desires a relationship of unity
with Him. We can compare this to the unity of marriage, where a couple becomes one but still remains
uniquely a man and a woman. This kind of relationship
is formed to differentiate from all other types of relationships. It is oneness within the marriage relationship that gives this couple deep intimacy. It becomes a
relationship where the couple knows one another better than anyone. If needed, they could make decisions
for each other and not be at odds in doing so.

Jesus in the garden of Gethsemane prays for the disciples in one of the most loving ways. It is also very clear of His love for the Father. He acknowledges that He would like for this "cup" to be not His but that the will of the Father is most desired to be done. Then He prays for the disciples to be one:

> John 17:11 (ESV), "And I am no longer in the world, but they are in the world, and I am coming to you. Holy Father, keep them in your name, which you have given me, that they may be one, even as we are one."

For us to understand this prayer point of Jesus, we need to understand the definition of one. Jesus is clear that He and the Father are one. He is asking that the Father make them, the disciples, one in the same way. A history lesson from the Old Testament is required here for us to understand the deep intimacy of Jesus and the Father who are one. We need word studies to understand the translated words in English because our language, for one, is most often associated with a numerical number for singular.

When I was an elementary school teacher, part of my job was teaching basic math. Children who are given plastic-colored cubes to count learn not only to count in the proper numerical order but also to associate each block with how many. By adding a block, the children would continue to add one more number value. So with this in mind, Jesus adding more disciples would mean growing in numbers. But we know that He is not talking about growing in numbers and is more so referring to one as unity. In other words, my elementary school students might have been given a stack of red blocks and the question would be more like, how many red piles do you see? The answer, of course, is one. It would not matter how many individual blocks but rather that the blocks were all the same. We understand this as unity because oneness is based on all things in common. We see this in the early church and expressed in the Acts of the church.

> Acts 4:32 (ESV), *"Now the full number of those who believed were of one heart and soul, and no one said that any of the things that belonged to him was his own, but they had everything in common."*

It is important to grasp unity as we consider that the Lord God is in perfect unity. The Father, Son, and Holy Spirit are in full agreement, and this is the oneness of the Trinity. It is not a contradiction between Jewish understanding in the Old Testament and the revealing of our Savior Jesus Christ. They are one Lord. For you and me, this is wildly important as we consider that Jesus prayed for His disciples to be one with the Father as He is. Agreement in every situation and agreement in absolute truth.

As we learn to pray, we are learning to be one with the Lord. We are learning to agree with Him and to move in ways that He moves. We cannot be at odds with God if we are truly one with Him.

When the birth of Jesus was announced in Bethlehem, Luke says the angels proclaimed peace to those whom God is pleased with (Luke 2:11–14), and Isaiah who prophesied the coming Christ child said, *"For to us a child is born, to us a son is given, and the government shall be upon his shoulder ... Wonderful Counselor, Mighty God, Everlasting Father, Prince of Peace"* (Isaiah 9:6, ESV).

These passages tell us that peace between God and man would come so that no longer would man be at war with God and no longer would God be at war with those whom He favors. He was offering us peace as He provided the Savior for all. It is interesting that Jesus in John 14:27 (ESV), as He is preparing the disciples for the coming crucifixion, says to them, *"Peace I leave with you; my peace I give to you. Not as the world gives do I give to you. Let not your hearts be troubled, neither let them be afraid."* This amazing peace is because we are given the opportunity to believe in Him and to be at peace with Him. Our prayer lives and the life we live, because of transforming prayer, is one where we become one with the Lord, and in that unity, we are at peace with His leadership, His ways.

Deep intimacy with God means that we are entering into a life where we live at peace with God, with others, and even within ourselves. This change and peace come as we begin to see life the way He sees it. We grow into that marriage of the Lamb referred to into Revelation 19. Until that day, we are promised to Him as a bride. This means we are finding oneness with Him so that on the day of the wedding feast, we are indeed aligned and in agreement with the One that is above it all.

To know God and to develop a relationship of intimacy with Him is to become people who are at peace with Him as He is with us. We may lack understanding in many situations, but we can still be completely confident that God will make good decisions for all of us. His leadership and kingdom are vitally important if we are to take care of it until His return. Can He trust us and will He find faith when He returns?

I remember being at my cousin's house over a college break and my oldest brother had told me he would come visit me there. I was sitting up late at night, waiting for him to arrive, when my cousin told me I should go to bed. She said she did not think he was coming and that there was no need for me to wait up. I responded kindly but with great confidence that if my brother told me he would come, then he would. Everything in me believed. I sat and waited in the living room and then around midnight there was a knock on the door. My brother had arrived. Years later, I realized the spiritual lesson the Lord had given me. Our intimacy with Christ is one that believes He will do what He says. We are able to wait upon Him even when others cannot. Intimacy with God produces a deep knowing of His plans and His Word. We can wait until midnight when others fall asleep because we know that our God will faithfully keep His Word. We act in confidence. We do not go to bed and fall asleep.

Intimacy with God is the natural part of a relationship with Him. Shadrach, Meshach, and Abednego knew this even in a land where idols and men were worshiped. Their response to worshiping any other god was refusal even though the punishment was death. Their response is tremendously intimate as they respond to King Nebuchadnezzar, *"If this be so, our God whom we serve is able to deliver us from the burning fiery furnace, and he will deliver us out of your hand, O king"* (Daniel 3:17, ESV). These men fully knew how God would respond and with full confidence, they refused to worship any other god and waited upon the Lord to deliver them. This, of course, becomes a sign to the king and Nebuchadnezzar responds with how powerful their God is and attributes it to the trust of the three men. Trust is a wonderful attribute of those who are intimate with God. We trust Him because we know His character.

In fact, trust is not the only fruit of our intimate lives but rather the fruit of the Spirit is exactly what is produced in an intimate relationship with God. We develop love, joy, peace, patience, kindness, goodness, faithfulness, gentleness, and self-control (Galatians 5:22–23) as we become intimate with God. You might be thinking, *These attributes are those of God and how could they be attributes in us?* Oneness. When we become one with Him, we look like Him and we act like Him.

Our prayer lives are the daily catalyst for transformation. The more we pray according to His will, with agreement toward His ways, we are transformed and given the mind of Christ and the Holy Spirit makes us one with Him. We step into unity. If He wants to curse an unfruitful fig tree (Mark 11) or if He wants to heal the sick or raise the dead (Matthew 10), then so do we.

To be intimate with God is to obey Him. Our obedience brings Him into view for others and for them to see Him instead of us. Our name and status die, and His name and leadership as King of Kings is revealed. Intimacy produces the power and truth to set others free. We do what the Father would do. Jesus said, "If you love me, you will keep my commandments" (John 14:15, ESV) and He promised that the Helper would never leave us, that the Father would love us, and that They would make Their home with us. Love and obedience flow from intimacy.

Love is the absolute expression of our intimate relationship with God.

"Beloved, let us love one another, for love is from God, and whoever loves has been born of God and knows God. Anyone who does not love does not know God, because God is love" (1 John 4:7–8, ESV).

Love in us means we know Him. His love in us allows us to actually flow in love toward Him and others. Love is the fullest expression of our intimate lives with Christ in us. We are able to love the way the Father loves. When we seek intimacy with God, we need to submit ourselves to being changed by love, and so often this means we need to choose love above all the other human feelings that might want to be first in our lives. It is learning to humble ourselves, as so many verses encourage us to do, so that we can choose His will above our own. Choosing to be changed by the Holy Spirit and choosing to agree that God's way is the best way does not always feel good or is not always understood at first but then we see Him show up and reveal Himself through us. Once we have acted in a manner that shows we are one with Him, we are changed.

Intimacy is the place in which we look forward to the promises of God coming as we hold on to them, and with great expectation, we pray to see the fulfillment of these promises come. Confidence in Him to keep His Words is the hope that is carried inside of us. We can release that hope to the world around us. Prayer is only a method or routine if it is not stewarded by an intimate relationship with God. It is my desire that all of us learn to pray but not for our glory. I hope that prayer is because we want the Lord Jesus Christ to receive His glory. Learning to release His kingdom through prayer is a necessary function of relationship with God and one that produces love, obedience, trust, and holy fruit. May we all grow in love with God and see His will done on earth just as it is in heaven.

Endnotes

1 "Strong's H6419 – *pālal. Blue Letter Bible*
   <https://www.blueletterbible.org/lexicon/h6419/
   esv/wlc/0-1/>

2 "Silent and Solo: How Americans Pray." 2017. *Barna
   Group*
   <https://www.barna.com/research/silent-solo-
   americans-pray/>

3 Ibid.

4 Ibid.

5 Ibid.

6 "Prayer in America: A Detailed Analysis of the
   Various Dimensions of Prayer." Paul Froese and
   Jeremy E. Uecker. 2022. *Journal for the Scientific Study
   of Religion*
   <https://doi.org/10.1111/jssr.12810>

www.ingramcontent.com/pod-product-compliance
Ingram Content Group UK Ltd.
Pitfield, Milton Keynes, MK11 3LW, UK
UKHW020711010925

7661UKWH00018B/132